Contents

Acknowledgements

Thanks to Colin Bent, Trainer Consultant in BAAF Southern England, and Florence Merredew, BAAF Health Group Development Officer, for their reading of the manuscript and helpful comments.

Note about the authors

For most of his professional life, **Dr Dan Hughes** has been a clinician specialising in the treatment of children and young people with severe emotional and behavioural problems. His treatment is family-centred, with the parents actively involved in their child's treatment, as well as addressing their own attachment histories. Working primarily with fostered and adopted children and their carers and parents, Dan borrowed heavily from attachment, intersubjectivity, and trauma theories and research to develop a model of treatment that he calls Dyadic Developmental Psychotherapy – also known as Attachment-Focused Family Therapy. Dan is the author of a number of books and articles including: *Building the Bonds of Attachment* (2nd edn) (2006, Jason Aronson); *Attachment-Focused Parenting* (2009, WW Norton) and *Attachment-Focused Family Therapy Workbook* (2011, WW Norton). More recently, he has published a book of poetry, *It was that One Moment…* (2012, Worth Publishing) focusing on the children and families he has treated. In 2012, he has written *Brain-Based Parenting* with Jon Baylin (WW Norton) and *Creating Loving Connections*, with Kim Golding (Jessica Kingsley Publishers).

Dan's current passion is the training of therapists in his treatment model. He has provided therapist training throughout the US, UK, Canada and other countries for the past 15 years. He also provides ongoing supervision and consultation to various clinicians and agencies. Dan has initiated a certification program for therapists interested in becoming proficient in his model of treatment.
Dhughes202@comcast.net
www.danielhughes.org

Lorna Miles is an adoptive parent and has been a foster carer on and off for 25 years, specialising in therapeutic foster care for the past seven years. In addition, she has worked with children in care in a variety of settings. She is involved in training foster carers, and since the publication of *Holding on and Hanging in* by BAAF in 2010, she has been running workshops on attachment.
www.lornamiles.co.uk

Jess and Paul Gethin are the adoptive parents of a sibling group of five children. Recognising that parenting children who have experienced early trauma can be very challenging, they initiated and ran a support group for adoptive parents on behalf of a local authority. Jess has received training from the Institute of Arts and Therapy in Education where she learnt a lot about the value of play and art in helping children with attachment difficulties and early trauma. Paul is a trustee of an adoption support agency.

The series editor
The editor of this series, **Hedi Argent**, is an established author/editor for BAAF. Her books cover a wide range of family placement topics; she has written several guides and a story book for young children.

Looking behind the label...

Jack has mild learning difficulties and displays some characteristics of ADHD and it is uncertain whether this will increase...

Beth and Mary both have a diagnosis of global developmental delay...

Abigail's birth mother has a history of substance abuse. There is no clear evidence that Abigail was prenatally exposed to drugs but her new family will have to accept some kind of developmental uncertainty...

Jade has some literacy and numeracy difficulties, but has made some improvement with the support of a learning mentor...

Prospective adopters and carers are often faced with the prospect of having to decide whether they can care for a child with a health need or condition they know little about and have no direct experience of. No easy task...

Will Jack's learning difficulties become more severe?
Will Beth and Mary be able to catch up?
When will it be clear whether or not Abigail has been affected by parental substance misuse?
And will Jade need a learning mentor throughout her school life?

It can be difficult to know where to turn for reliable information. What lies behind the diagnoses and "labels" that many looked after children bring with them? And what will it be like to live with them? How will they benefit from family life?

Parenting Matters is a unique series, "inspired" by the terms used – and the need to "decode them" – in profiles of children needing new permanent families. Each title provides expert knowledge about a particular condition, coupled with facts, figures and guidance presented in a straightforward and accessible style. Each book also describes what it is like to parent an affected child, with adopters and foster carers "telling it like it is", sharing their parenting experiences, and offering useful advice; some of these cases are more recent than others, and it is useful to remember that professional practice in the past is not what it is today. This combination of expert information and first-hand experiences will help readers to gain understanding, and to make informed decisions.

Titles in the series will deal with a wide range of health conditions and steer readers to where they can get more information. They will offer a sound introduction to the topic under consideration and offer a glimpse of what it would be like to live with a "labelled" child. Most importantly, this series will look behind the label and give families the confidence to look more closely at a child whom they otherwise might have passed by.

Keep up with new titles as they are published by signing up to our newsletter on www.corambaaf.org.uk/bookshop.

Shaila Shah

Titles in this series include:

- *Parenting a Child with Attention Deficit Hyperactivity Disorder*

- *Parenting a Child with Dyslexia*

- *Parenting a Child with Mental Health Issues*

- *Parenting a Child Affected by Parental Substance Misuse*

Introduction

This book is concerned with emotional and behavioural difficulties and the special needs of children, particularly adopted and looked after children, who have these difficulties.

The first half of the book starts with a short explanation of emotional and behavioural difficulties and what these terms mean for children: symptoms, prognosis and treatment are outlined clearly and simply. It goes on to look at the different ways in which emotional and behavioural difficulties can affect child development; the issues these conditions raise with regard to educational provision for affected children; and where and how to get help for children with these issues.

The second half of the book tells the stories of Lorna Miles and Jess and Paul Gethin, and their experiences of parenting children with emotional and behavioural difficulties and how this affected day-to-day family life.

UNDERSTANDING EMOTIONAL AND BEHAVIOURAL DIFFICULTIES

DAN HUGHES

CHAPTER 1

What are emotional and behavioural difficulties?

When a child is raised in conditions of safety and is fully engaged in relationships with his caregivers, that child is likely to show the increasing **organisation** of all aspects of his development. This leads to a coherent and integrated sense of self that enables him to make sense of his world and interact with others in a competent, enjoyable, and successful manner. However, when the child does not experience safety and rewarding relationships, his development will be **disorganised**. This means that his functioning – whether it be behavioural, emotional, cognitive or all of these – is likely to be dysregulated, impulsive, non-reflective, and tending toward the extremes of rigidity or chaos.

When a child begins life in an environment where his most basic developmental needs are not being adequately met, that child is at great risk of developing significant emotional and behavioural problems. There is an overwhelming body of research that indicates that abuse and neglect leave a child at risk of a wide range of mental health diagnoses. These include:

- anxiety and mood disorders;
- Attention Deficit Hyperactivity Disorder (ADHD);
- oppositional-defiant disorder;
- conduct disorder; and
- disorders of relationship including the attachment relationship.

There is reason to believe that these various difficulties/disorders all reflect an underlying lack of organisation of the child's behavioural, emotional, and cognitive functioning.

It is not surprising that the disorganisation of the developing self and the resultant emotional and behavioural difficulties are highly influenced by the child's early attachment relationship (their emotional bond) with parents or carers. When the child's attachment is secure, his developing self is integrated and organised. When the child's attachment is disorganised, his developing self is also disorganised.

Attachment disorganisation is a research classification given to a high percentage of children who have early histories of abuse and neglect. Attachment disorganisation in early childhood is a risk factor for mental illness in adolescence and adulthood. Attachment researchers Sroufe and colleagues (2005) propose that the wide range of symptoms that characterise emotional and behavioural difficulties can be understood as reflecting a lack of organisation – or integration – of the child's emotional, cognitive and behavioural functioning. It is certain to present great difficulties for a child to develop organised attachment patterns with his caregivers, if these same caregivers are abusing, neglecting, and/or abandoning him.

SECTION I

CHAPTER 2

Symptoms, prognosis and treatment

Symptoms

Rather than expand on the various diagnoses of children
with emotional and behavioural difficulties mentioned
in the previous chapter, which are often seen in children
with histories of intrafamilial, interpersonal trauma, I will
instead summarise the symptoms that are characteristic of a
proposed new diagnosis for these children: **Developmental
Trauma Disorder** (Cook et al, 2005). While this is not yet
a formal diagnosis, there is consensus among a great many
child trauma experts that children exposed to abuse and
neglect are at risk in the following domains of impairment.

A. Attachment
Avoidant, anxious, and especially disorganised patterns make it
difficult for the child to seek comfort and support, accept guidance
and direction, communicate openly, and develop the safety

necessary to explore the world and develop autonomy.

B. Biology
The child has difficulty recognising and regulating basic biological processes of appetite, sleep, and elimination, as well as sensory integration and hygiene needs.

C. Emotional regulation
The child has difficulty identifying, regulating, and expressing various emotional states such as anger, fear, sadness, and shame as well as excitement and joy.

D. Dissociation
The child has a tendency to withdraw into imagination and fantasy and disengage from the here-and-now environment in response to many stressors; the child at times may engage in behaviours about which she has little awareness.

E. Behaviour control
The child is at risk of frequent impulsivity, hyper-reactivity to stress, compulsions, explosiveness, hyperactivity, or passive and withdrawn states.

F. Cognition
The child has poor attention and concentration, obsessions, misperceptions, negative assumptions about the motives of others, poor ability to reflect on the inner life (thoughts, feelings, intentions, wishes) of both self and others.

G. Self-concept
The child has a poorly defined sense of self and/or a rigidly negative sense of self, and lack of continuity of sense of self from one situation to the next, making transitions very difficult.

Prognosis

While the majority of fostered and adopted children are able to attain sufficient emotional and behavioural maturation, reflecting a level of functioning in most areas that is within the normal range, nevertheless the risk that these children will not attain such a level is considerably higher than it is in the general population.

The probability of a favourable prognosis is affected by:

- the duration and severity of the history of abuse and neglect;

- the severity of symptoms;

- the presence of relationships and experiences that can facilitate resilience; and

- internal strengths and resources.

Providing these children with a stable, permanent placement (ideally a family home) where the child is helped to develop secure attachment relationships with primary caregivers is central in any efforts to facilitate healing, trauma resolution, and developmental progress.

Treatment

Treatment for fostered and adopted children with behavioural and emotional difficulties needs to be comprehensive and integrative if the causes are to be addressed and the interventions are to be thorough. It is crucial that the foster carers or adoptive parents are actively engaged in the child's treatment in order to facilitate the child's attachment security with her carers and parents, as well as to provide the child with comfort and support as she explores issues of terror and shame that emerge from her past and continue to affect her functioning.

There are six core components of treatment that have been recommended by the Child Trauma Task Force in the US (Cook *et al*, 2005).

I. Safety
This is the foundation of any successful treatment. Treatment needs to aid the child's ability to experience safety in both her home and school if she is to benefit from the environment provided. Her emotional and behavioural difficulties often represent a lack of a sense of safety and when she begins to feel safe with the adults who provide for her care, these difficulties are likely to decrease. As her safety increases, she is also likely to be able to better participate in, and benefit from, her treatment.

2. Self-regulation
Regulation problems are often central to the child's emotional and behavioural difficulties. In secure attachment relationships, the child first learns to regulate her emotions and behaviour through co-regulation of her inner states with her parents or carers. Only then is the self-regulation of her emotions and behaviours likely to develop well. When a parent or carer who is with a child in a stressful situation (whether it be an event associated with a past memory, a conflict, an act of discipline, or a failure) remains regulated, the child is much less likely to become dysregulated in that situation. Once the child's ability to co-regulate her emotional and behavioural state with her caregiver is established, she is much more likely to benefit from cognitive strategies for self-regulation.

3. Self-reflection
Children with histories of abuse and neglect as well as attachment disruptions or disorganisation are likely to have poor reflective abilities. They have difficulties knowing what they think, feel, and want, as well as knowing what their parents or carers think,

feel, and want. Reflective skills are central in mental health and are associated with attachment security. They are aided through interactions and dialogue with reflective adults who are able to communicate acceptance for, not judgment of, the inner life of the child, and restrict evaluations to the child's behaviours.

4. Traumatic experience integration

The child's traumatic history, involving abuse, neglect, abandonment, and loss, needs to be integrated into her life story in order to reduce its ongoing negative impact on her life. The child needs assistance in making sense of the meaning of the traumas, while regulating the emotions associated with them – especially terror and shame – and understanding their connections to her current life. The supportive and comforting presence of her emotionally strong parents or carers will greatly assist her in being able to proceed through this difficult work.

5. Relational engagement

Intra-familial, interpersonal trauma places the child at high risk for having considerable difficulty relating with her parents, therapist, teachers and others in reciprocal dialogue, co-operation, sharing, and accepting guidance and limits. Treatment involves facilitating engagement with a child who is unwilling or unable to be positively engaged. The therapist works as actively with the adults in the child's life as with the child herself to increase the adult's ability to remain engaged with an oppositional, angry, or withdrawn, avoidant child.

6. Positive affect enhancement

Children who have not learned how to regulate their emotional states are likely to have as much trouble regulating positive emotions as they do regulating negative emotions. They are not comfortable with excitement, joy, or affection and tend to avoid or become anxious when exposed to events that would elicit those emotions. Praise is likely to be very anxiety-provoking. Treatment

SECTION I

involves exposing these children to such positive experiences gradually, in small amounts, co-regulating the emotion, and reflecting on these new experiences.

CHAPTER 3

Frequently asked questions

Even if his emotional and behavioural problems originated in his early years, why doesn't he just get over it?

If we reply 'He would if he could', you are likely to think, 'But he can. Some days he handles his anger so much better. Sometimes he tells the truth when he does something wrong.' Yes, and some days we stick with our diet from morning till night. And some days we keep the sarcasm out of our voice when our partner does something that annoys us. What is wrong with the 'Some days he can' argument?

First, habits are hard to change, especially habits of a social–emotional nature. When habits develop in conditions of safety – a child has loving parents whom he can trust to meet his needs and who remain present in conditions of stress – this child is likely to turn to his parents for comfort and assistance and to trust their judgments when they direct him to do something that he would rather not do. But habits formed when a child is living in conditions of abuse and neglect are likely to involve this child trying to meet his own needs, since he cannot trust his parents to do so. This child is likely to rely much more on deceit, manipulation, intimidation, and on isolating himself from adults who might make things more difficult for him. These are habits developed to survive without a caregiver.

Either set of habits represent changes in the structure and functioning of the human brain and central nervous system that are developing to best manage the world that the young child finds himself in. The brain of the abused or neglected child is wired to survive a world where there is no adult to guide, enjoy, and protect him. While he might have such parents around now, his brain does not know what to do with them – how to trust them, communicate with them, seek them out when in distress, and even be open to learning from them.

So why does your child do well only on certain days? And why do you keep to your diet only on certain days? The answer to that is not yet covered in the books that address many aspects of human development. On some days our complex social, emotional, physical, cognitive, and values systems are organised in our brain in a manner for us to experience our wish for improved health and appearance sufficiently to maintain our diet. On those days, we truly "want" to diet because of the strong sense of our goals, which are experienced as being more important than the delicious taste of a dessert or a roast dinner and more important than the comfort that we find in taking a second helping. On other days, we "want" the immediate deep pleasure that comes from enjoying a particular meal or snack.

On both days we are doing what we "want" to do, not what we "should" do. Possibly we give ourselves too much credit for staying with our diet. On days when it is hard, perhaps we simply have the mental flexibility and focus to move our goals for the sake of our health and appearance to a higher spot in our decision-making that overrides the enjoyment of food. But this takes quite a bit of neurological maturity, involving areas of the dorsolateral prefrontal cortex (part of the brain involved in the regulation of actions) that are not yet mature in the child and adolescent. These areas of the brain are not fully developed until a person is in his mid-20s.

So, your child is not likely to be able to "get over it" consistently, because of how his brain developed in his early years in response to abuse and neglect, the fact that his brain is not yet fully mature, and how emotional and behavioural habits that developed in earlier circumstances are hard to consistently change.

Isn't there wisdom in the saying "Let sleeping dogs lie"?

It might be wise to let a dead dog lie, but not a sleeping dog, because he is likely to wake up at the most inappropriate time – namely, when he is startled and ready to attack or run. If we want a child to be safe, truly safe, then we have to help him to be safe within his own mind and brain. If there are parts of his brain that are still strongly associated with terror and shame, then your child will never be safe because many events in his life are likely to trigger those parts of the brain to awaken. We cannot protect the child from these events, which might be on the television, in a song, associated with a sound, smell, or the sight of a particular car or hat or beard.

Why, then, do we want so much to believe in the value of "letting sleeping dogs lie"? Because when we awaken past memories, the child is likely to become distressed. He may cry, become angry, be very sad or filled with shame. He may try hard not to think about

SECTION I

these things and devote much of his energy to avoiding those memories. We may feel that we should respect his wishes. But he is likely to be unsuccessful, and when his present life is causing him some anxiety and frustration, the likelihood that these old memories will become more active only becomes greater.

We should not force a child to confront the "demons" from his past. But when they are close to the surface, being activated by some recent events or behaviours, we should be available to assist him in addressing them. When he is with those adults with whom he feels safe, he is in the best position to manage any strong emotion associated with certain events as well as to begin to make sense of those events in a way that reduces the terror and shame associated with them.

There is a second reason why we might be tempted to "let sleeping dogs lie" – this involves the distress that we feel when our child is in distress. When we love a child, it causes us distress when we experience his fears and shame. We tend to want to make it go away, distract him from it, so we convince ourselves that it is better for him to be content and happy now and focus on what he has at this time, rather than what happened to him or what he did not have in previous years. When we realise that the pain will not go away permanently but will most likely just become worse, because it causes the child to avoid and not manage situations that he needs to learn to address and understand better, then we may find the emotional strength needed to be with the child in his distress rather than try to sweep it under the carpet.

Closely related to this reason is that the child's "sleeping dogs" may remind the adults of their own sleeping dogs that they have managed to avoid addressing over the years. An adult may be triggered by her child's focus on incidents of abuse and neglect because of their similarity with events from the adult's own attachment history. If a child was physically abused by his father and begins to cry about it, this might well remind the adult of her own father emotionally or verbally abusing her when she was a child. If the adult has never managed to sort out the emotions and thoughts associated with certain events in her own childhood, then she is likely to avoid – and want the child to avoid – speaking of similar events that cause him great distress. While we may have been able to let our sleeping dogs lie and still have a reasonably satisfying and productive life, the severity of the child's abuse and neglect history may well make it impossible to follow the same strategy.

If abuse and neglect is so damaging to a child's emotional and behavioural development, does this suggest that the situation is now hopeless?

Definitely not. While the abuse and neglect are not easily managed and resolved, it is certainly possible for the child to do so over time with the active help of his caregivers or adoptive parents.

Abuse and neglect definitely influence the development of the structure and functioning of the brain. However, the brain resists rigidity and tends to remain capable of change throughout a person's entire life. The prefrontal cortex, where much of the social, emotional, and behavioural learning that this chapter has covered are centred, tends to be one of the most plastic (capable of changing) areas of the brain. This area is most influenced by relationships, especially the relationships the child has with his parents and caregivers – his attachment figures (Siegel, 2011). If the child's birth parents were the source of the abuse and neglect and subsequent maladaptive brain development, the new learning that is necessary – and possible – is most likely to emerge from the child's relationship with his new adoptive parents or caregivers, who provide safety and positive meanings about the self and other, for the child.

Why does he seem to get worse when we praise him?

The first reason is that the core of our relationship with our partner, parent or child needs to be based on acceptance, not evaluations. When children do not feel accepted for who they are, instead of experiencing praise safely, they will experience it as pressure to be good or do well. They believe that they are liked and wanted because they are good or do well, not because they are who they are. Many fostered and adopted children do not feel accepted for who they are.

A second reason is that children who have been abused and neglected make sense of that maltreatment by blaming themselves for it. How else could a two-year-old make sense of his parent hitting him, swearing at him and ignoring him? He must be bad. This belief represents the child's sense of shame – he is bad, worthless and/or unlovable. With such a negative self-concept, praise does not fit his sense of who he is. As a result, it makes him anxious and often motivated to prove his parents or carers wrong in their praise of him. He does not deserve the praise.

A third reason why children may not be comfortable with praise is our motive for praising. If a child senses that we are praising him because we believe that praise will induce him to act in that way again, he is likely to resist the praise. If we praise a person because we want her to change her behaviour from negative to positive and she reads our motive accurately, she will be less motivated to change. She will feel that she is being manipulated and that you do not really mean your praise. Think of how you would respond to your partner if you thought that his or her motive for praising you was primarily to induce you to do it again. This is not to suggest that you should not praise your child. The following are ways where praise might be helpful for your child to develop a more positive view of self and more positive habits.

- Firstly, be sure that the great majority of your interactions with your child are based on acceptance, not evaluations, which are central to both praise and criticism. If most of the time you are with your child, you are simply enjoying your time together, interested in what he is doing or what you are doing together, and getting to know each other without judgment, then periodic praise is likely to be of benefit for your child's development.

- Secondly, praise is likely to be more effective when your intention is simply to share your positive experience of what your child has done or about your time with him. Your intention is not to get him to repeat an act. (If you do not praise him in order to get him to do it again, he is actually more likely to do it again.)

- Thirdly, praise is more likely to be effective when it is a spontaneous expression of delight, of being impressed, of your experience of something very meaningful for you about what your child is doing. This tends to be expressed nonverbally more than verbally. Your voice conveys enthusiasm and delight, as do your facial expressions, and your gestures and movements. Much less effective praise is conveyed in a tone that is judgmental – when you are deciding that the behaviour is "good".

SECTION I

I'm sure that he does things just to make me mad. Why would he do that?

You may be correct that at times one of your child's motives for his behaviour is to make you angry. At the same time, he may also have other motives. He may be anxious, sad, or feeling shame and does not know how to manage that emotion by seeking or accepting support from you. He shows his distress through anger, because he is unable to express more vulnerable emotions, or because doing so makes him feel uncomfortable.

Also, somehow he knows that his attachment figure – his caregiver – should keep him safe and his habitual distress makes him feel unsafe. In a basic way, he may blame you for his not feeling safe and so be angry with you – it is your fault. If – in his mind – you are causing him distress, he will retaliate by causing you distress.

A second reason is likely to relate to his shame. He may well perceive himself as being bad and unlovable and has grown to expect interactions with adults and children that confirm this sense of himself. He may actually become comfortable with negative interactions since they fit his basic sense of self. Positive interactions make him anxious or somehow do not meet his wish for attention and recognition since they do not fit his model of himself. Thus, he may be preventing your signs of love and joy directed toward him by ensuring that you are angry with him for a good deal of the time.

A third reason is the notion of "payback". He may experience routine discipline or the fact that you do not have as much time to devote to him as he wishes as a sign of your not caring for him, being mean to him, or wanting to make him angry, so – in his mind – he responds in kind.

Finally, many fostered and adopted children with histories of abuse and neglect seem to seek angry interactions from the female carer or mother more than from the male carer or father. This tends to be the case even if the male caregiver does most of the childcare and most of the disciplining. I believe that central to this common occurrence is the child's fear of nurturing, cuddles and unconditional love, which are more often associated with the mother. When the child was an infant and toddler, he did want nurture – he was desperate for it – but seldom experienced it. The pain of not being nurtured led him to not seek it, and then to actively avoid it. When the new mother offers nurture, the child becomes frightened by it, not trusting it. The best way to manage any emerging wish to be nurtured is to remain angry with his mother and also to act in a way to make her angry with her child, and so withdraw her nurture.

He always says that he doesn't know what he thinks or feels or why he does something. Is he telling the truth or just avoiding facing and talking about what he's done?

It is very likely that he is telling the truth. Children with histories of abuse/neglect and attachment problems and losses tend to have few words to describe what they think, feel, want or why they do things. Your child is likely to be as puzzled as you are about the motives underlying his behaviour. He may answer your questions with the reason someone gave him for his behaviour in the past (e.g. 'I didn't try hard enough') or he may use a common excuse ('I forgot'; 'I didn't mean to'; 'She started it').

He may also avoid thinking about why he does things because he has a fundamental assumption that he misbehaves because he is bad, lazy, selfish or unlovable. He may constantly view himself under the light of shame. If he was to honestly try hard to make sense of his behaviour, he would probably conclude each time that he did it because he is bad or stupid or "not normal".

Your child also won't want to try to talk about his motives for his behaviour if you are angry, annoyed, or disappointed in him at the time. This will lead him to respond to your negative emotion about his behaviour in a very defensive, self-protective way, which is likely to interfere with your keeping an open mind about what just happened. He will probably perceive your anger about his behaviour as rejection and dislike for who he is as a person, no matter what words you use to discuss the event. You are much more likely to elicit his co-operation to talk about what happened if you approach him when you have become calm and have openly engaged with him. Even then, it is best not to assume a monotone, stern voice characteristic of a lecture, as this will cause him to feel evaluated, judged and disapproved of, regardless of your words. It is much better to speak in a more natural, relaxed manner with modulations and rhythms in your voice, conveying that you are describing and exploring an event without evaluating the reasons for it. You are discussing it to understand it, not to judge it.

You tell me that he needs my empathy and understanding because of his difficult past. When will someone have some empathy and understanding for me?

That is an excellent and important question. If you do not experience that someone truly understands and feels empathy for your situation of trying to parent or care for your child when he is constantly fighting against your care, then it will be much harder for you to continue to care well for your child. You are not a robot. You have your own feelings and doubts. You become angry, discouraged, and at times experience shame over your failure to be more successful as a parent. You feel all alone in your efforts.

If, after months or years, you see little progress in spite of your efforts to care for your child in a manner that will reduce his emotional and behavioural problems, you are likely to begin to lose hope that things will ever be any different. By then you may well feel that caring for your child is just a job. You will do it. You will do it adequately. You may try to do it well at times. But you will have lost your sense of warmth, care, compassion and joy that you used to have for this child or that you have for your other children. You may lose interest in your child and find little positive meaning in your interactions with him. In these circumstances, it becomes very hard to continue to provide him with the empathy and understanding that you are being told he needs.

For you to be able to keep your mind and heart open to your child so that you can remain engaged with him, you need to know that others are engaged with you in this way: your partner, your best friend, and hopefully a trusted professional – a therapist or social worker – has empathy for you, understands you and your challenges, and accepts you for who you are. And who are you? A good person. A person who is doing the best that you can to help your child. A person who deeply cares for your child, or – if the sense of caring has become weak – strongly wants to be able to care again. Yes, you do need to experience empathy if you are parenting a child who also needs to experience empathy from you.

CHAPTER **4**

Specific parenting tasks

This chapter lists and explores some specific parenting tasks that can be undertaken with children who have emotional and behavioural difficulties in order to help them to improve their behaviour and increase their self-esteem.

Work to remain open and engaged with your child rather than defensive. Over time, this will help her to become open and engaged rather than aggressive or defensive.

We know that our bodies have a way of synchronising with each other. If one person coughs or scratches his head, the person next to them also tends to do it. The same is true for our emotions: one person who is angry or sad tends to make other people around them angry or sad. Similarly, if one person approaches another in an open and engaged manner, that person also tends to become open and engaged. If one person is defensive, those around them become defensive. When your interaction with your child begins, if she is defensive, you will tend to become defensive yourself. If you are able to inhibit that tendency and remain open and engaged, she is likely to become open and engaged too. This may take a number of repetitions over time, but is likely to be effective in the long run.

Maintain an attitude of PACE (Playfulness, Acceptance, Curiosity, Empathy).

This attitude tends to be very helpful if you are to be successful in remaining open and engaged with your child (Hughes, 2009; Golding and Hughes, 2012). These four traits are similar to the attitude that we routinely maintain with infants.

A. Playfulness

Playfulness conveys a state of active enjoyment when with another person. This state is easier for many abused children to experience than is affection. It conveys a sense of lightness and hope: the conflict or problem behaviour is not too big for us to manage. We will get through this together. Playfulness also helps abused or neglected children to become used to positive emotional experiences. Often, positive emotions can cause them to become dysregulated — they can become anxious and avoidant when they begin to experience joy, excitement or love. Experiencing playfulness gives them a break from the hard times in their lives. Neurologically, when we are laughing, it is very difficult to feel shame. Finally, a playful attitude facilitates the development of your child's sense of humour. As this develops, she is less likely to feel that others are making fun of her and will be more able to see other perspectives.

B. Acceptance

Acceptance conveys a sense that you accept your child, although you may evaluate her behaviour. Your child is your child, for better or for worse. Sometimes you become angry at what she does, but not at what she thinks, feels, or wants. Her inner life is not evaluated, but unconditionally accepted. If she thinks that you do not like her, if she feels hatred toward you, if she wishes that she could live with someone else, she is not judged when she tells you. If she is judged, she will not tell you, and she will not "use her words". If her inner life is accepted and then met with an open and engaged response of empathy and curiosity, it is much more likely to change than if it is met with anger and shame-inducing comments. For example:

Child: I don't think that you like me!

Parent: Thanks for telling me! That must be hard for you if you think that I don't like you. Very hard, if your own parent doesn't like you!

Child: Sometimes I don't think that you do.

Parent: Oh, how difficult that must be for you! Help me to understand: what do I say or do that makes you think that I don't like you?

C. Curiosity

Curiosity is a non-knowing and non-judgmental stance toward your child's inner life. It stems from a deep desire to understand your child: her thoughts, feelings, wishes and intentions; her memories, values, judgments and perceptions. Curiosity conveys a sense that you are deeply interested in your child. You are fascinated with who she is. You want to discover who she is. You are gazing underneath your child's behaviour in order to better understand it before judging it.

Curiosity is **not**: 'You did that because you are just being selfish'.

Here, the parent assumes that his child's inner life is known by him and he judges it negatively.

Curiosity is **not**: 'Why did you do that?' This is said in anger. It conveys that we might not know the exact reason, but we know that whatever it is, we don't like it.

Curiosity **is**: 'I wonder why you did that? Any ideas?' This conveys an open and engaged stance, with a desire to understand, not judge, your child's inner life. If your child says that she does not know why she did it – which she is likely to do, because she tends not to know – you might respond with, 'Well, why don't we try to figure it out? Then we will know what to do about what you did.'

D. Empathy

Empathy refers to your staying with your child in her emotional state and experiencing it with her. Through empathy, you are conveying that you deeply understand her emotions and that you are supporting and comforting her over the stress that she is feeling. In conveying empathy for her current emotional state – even one that you created by criticising her behaviour, or one that she created through a poor choice – you are joining her in her distress. This is the first and often most important part of your efforts to help her to learn from the experience itself and consider other choices for her behaviour. Skipping empathy and moving right into giving advice and problem-solving is likely to create a defensive state in your child so that she is less likely to be open to your guidance.

Search for the strengths that lie within her and communicate your experiences of these strengths.

Your experience of your child is at its most powerful when

it is conveyed in your voice, facial expressions, gestures and movements rather than simply with words.

If a child has many challenging and difficult behaviours, our tendency is to focus on them. Eventually the danger is that we will see only her "problems", and she will become a "problem child". Your challenge is to find – and not lose sight of – her strengths that lie under her problems, and then elicit and respond to those strengths.

Certainly, if she has strengths such as in sports, computers, a particular interest or academic subject, you need to recognise them and facilitate her progress. However, you will have an even bigger impact on her development if you are able to perceive the strengths that lie within her and beneath her problems. These might include:

- persistence;
- courage;
- a sense of fair play;
- compassion for someone weak or with a disability;
- gentleness with an animal;
- willingness to help a neighbour;
- a desire to be "normal";
- efforts to "fit in" with the other members of the family;
- a sense of humour;
- a desire to learn something; or
- a desire to share a quiet moment together.

You might think that she does not have any of these strengths — but she does, or she has similar ones. She might be good at hiding them. She might fear to show them because she will be laughed at (or so she imagines, in her mind). The strengths might be there, but be small, tentative. They might be there but seen only when she feels safe — and she does not feel safe very often.

If you notice an inner strength, be sure that she sees that you notice it and have a positive response to it. You might show your response with a smile, a touch on the arm or shoulder, an expression (Ah!), or quick comment ('That was lovely!'). Don't overdo it or she might become anxious, embarrassed, or feel pressure from you to do it more (even though you were not placing any pressure on her). Too many words may make her uncomfortable and might make her feel that you are "reinforcing" her. It is much more likely that she will believe your bodily expressions of delight or recognition of something about her than that she will believe something that you say.

Avoid stern monotones or lectures when addressing her behaviour.

Your child is more likely to listen well and stay engaged with you if you are able to express yourself in a modulated, rhythmic voice. This recommendation comes directly from neurological research, which demonstrates that a rhythmic voice activates an open and engaged state of interaction with another person, whereas a monotone voice activates a defensive state in which the child (or adult) focuses on self-protection rather than learning from the other person. It is when the child is in this open and engaged state that she is truly receptive to our guidance and directives. This interaction should be experienced as a dialogue in which the adult and child are receptive to each other's perspective rather than a monologue where only the adult's perspective is important.

SECTION I

Consequences tend to be more effective when you have first established a relationship that is based on safety, companionship and commitment.

Your child needs to know that the relationship she has with you is "for better or worse", before she will trust you enough to trust your motives for your acts of discipline.

Regretfully, there are many books on childcare and parenting that suggest that the foundations of discipline are consequences. These books stress that positive consequences work better than negative ones and that they should be given immediately so that the child will associate the behaviour with the consequence. Some stress that a consequence should apply to almost any behaviour – positive consequences for behaviours that we want to encourage and negative consequences for those that we want to discourage.

This is regretful because these books often assume that the child has a secure attachment to her parents. When such a relationship exists, consequences may well be an additional incentive to do something that the child would rather not do or to inhibit an action that she might want to do. But without a secure attachment relationship, your influence over your child through the use of consequences is likely to be greatly reduced.

Without this secure attachment relationship, sometimes, indeed, your child may behave in a certain way to get or to avoid a consequence that you have attached to her action. But at other times, she would rather not do what she is supposed to do, and so does not do it, regardless of the consequence. In fact, she might give herself a consequence that is much more "reinforcing" than the one that you might give her. She might deliberately defy you or break something of yours because she wants the "reward" of seeing you upset, sad, angry or anxious. She might misbehave because she wants to be isolated in her room because being alone is easier for her than learning to socialise. She might misbehave for the "reward" of not being allowed to go to an amusement park or football match because the excitement of such places makes her anxious. She might be more comfortable with negative consequences rather than positive ones because of her sense of shame and worthlessness.

Bringing a sense of safety, companionship and commitment to your relationship with your child is likely to have a much greater positive impact on her behaviour than the questionable impact of consequences.

When consequences are not effective, part of the problem may be that you do not know the reasons for her behaviours.

Reasons for behaviour are not excuses, in that your child is still responsible for her behaviour. However, if the consequences are not effective, it may be that you have not addressed the underlying reasons. If, for example, your child's behaviour reflects a fear that you are not committed to her, then finding ways to address and reduce that fear is likely to be the best way to address the behaviour.

Too often, we adopt a surface attitude in which our only goal is to change a child's behaviour. We do not care why the behaviour has occurred; we only want it to stop. With such an attitude, we are less likely to ensure that the behaviour remains stopped. If the reason for it has not been addressed, it is likely to recur. Over the years, the parents who have been the most successful in inducing their children to improve their behaviour, say 'I don't react to her behaviour any more. Instead, I first make sense of it, and then I respond to it.'

When a parent is under stress, that parent is more likely to focus on their child's behaviour and to be less interested in the reasons for the behaviour. Under stress, the mind tends to adopt an either/or perspective, with diminished interest in exploring complex reasons and shades of grey. This leads the parent toward a behavioural perspective with little interest in the context in which the child's behaviour occurred. Awareness of this underlines the value of parents taking care of themselves if they are to take care of their child in a manner that is less reactive.

Attachment deepens and becomes secure when your child is able to seek and accept your comfort and support.

Many fostered and adopted children with trauma and attachment problems have great difficulty in seeking comfort and support. They have developed a false security based on self-reliance, and turning to an adult for comfort is likely to activate memories of when they did so and received only rejection, ridicule or indifference.

When a child does not seek comfort and support from her parent, the parent is likely, over time, to experience the child's detachment as a rejection of them. It seems that the child does not need the parent and perceives him or her as a servant who does what the child wants. The parent may then experience the child as being a "boarder" in their home, and not as a son or daughter. If the parent is to be able to continue providing comfort and support when the child does not accept it, it is important that the parent has empathy for the child and her history. Empathy for the child means that the parent will understand that the reasons why she refuses parental comfort have nothing to do with the parent. It is also important for the parent to understand and accept his or her own frustration over the rejections, rather than descend into shame about it.

When your child is in distress, comfort and support should not be forced, but rather gently and persistently offered in a quiet voice, with a friendly facial expression. Just sitting near her with an empathetic attitude may gradually help her to accept comfort from you. Any efforts to touch or cuddle her are best done tentatively and lightly, and should be readily withdrawn at the first sign that they are not received well.

Be aware that your child is likely to experience a pervasive sense of shame that lies under her emotional and behavioural difficulties.

When a young child experiences abuse and neglect from her parents, she is almost certainly going to make sense of it by concluding that she is a bad child, worthless and unlovable. Shame makes it extremely difficult to face one's misbehaviours, causing your child to hide behind lies, excuses, blaming others, minimising what occurred and becoming enraged when you ask her to address it. The difficulties will not decrease and realistic guilt over actions that should cause distress will not increase, until shame has been greatly reduced.

To reduce shame, consider doing the following.

- Be careful to limit your criticism to your child's behaviours, not to her inner life. When correcting her behaviour, do not add an angry comment about what you guess to be the motives for her behaviour, such as 'You did that because you just wanted your own way!' Stay focused on the behaviour and leave any dialogue about possible reasons for it until both you and your child are no longer upset.

33

- Repair the relationship as soon as possible after the correction for the behaviour. Using relationship withdrawal as a form of discipline will only increase your child's fear of rejection and shame.

- When she is able, and with much support, explore with your child possible reasons for her misbehaviour. Your child may assume that she misbehaves because she is "bad" or "selfish" or "unlovable", but when she realises that there were other reasons for her behaviour (i.e. fear of loss, of not being liked, of not being attended to), this new understanding of her motives is likely to decrease shame. However, she cannot be talked into these new perspectives – she needs to be actively involved in their discovery.

- As her shame begins to decrease and she feels somewhat safer in her relationship with you, your child may begin to verbalise her experience of shame. She may be able to say: 'I'll never change, I'm just bad', or 'Why do you love me? I'm a bad girl', or 'I'm just bad and I'll never stop hurting you'. Such comments suggest that she is beginning to have some doubts about her sense of shame.

When your child verbalises her shame, it is important not to reassure or argue with her – this would only make her think that you do not really know her or that you are lying to her. A more helpful response will be to express empathy and then curiosity about her sense of shame. You could have discussions that might include some of the following responses:

When you do something wrong, you think that it's because you're bad! How hard that must be for you! How much that feeling must hurt!

I am so sorry that you feel that you are bad whenever you do something wrong! No wonder it is so hard for you to tell the truth.

Do you always feel that you are bad when you do something wrong? Do you ever think that there are other reasons? How long have you felt that way?

Do you think you first thought that when your dad was hurting you?

Your child might not experience her relationship with you as being "for better or worse".

If you are in a committed relationship with your partner, then you probably feel safe enough to know that when you have a disagreement or are separated for a while, the relationship will still continue. You know that the relationship will last because it is more important to you than any conflict or separation. With that trust, the conflict is less stressful as it does not pose a threat to your relationship.

If there are uncertainties about how committed you both are to the relationship, then you would be much more anxious when the relationship is not going well. The safety that comes from the belief that the relationship will continue becomes precarious.

Children who are securely attached to their parents have a similar sense that the relationship is "for better or worse". They know that anger, conflicts and separations will not damage the relationship. No matter how big the anger and conflict, they never worry that the relationship might end.

However, when children have been abused, neglected, and/or have lived in a number of foster homes or similar placements, they do not make the "for better or worse" assumption. They live in dread that this conflict or their latest misbehaviour will be the one that ends the relationship. They often believe that when they return from school or wake up in the morning, they will find that their "bags will be packed". Promising your child that this relationship is permanent is not likely to convince her if she is still filled with shame or if she has had a number of moves. Reassurance will not help. Staying with her in her fears and doubts with empathy, while giving her lived experiences with you over the months and years, is likely to be the only way for her to trust that the relationship is "for better or worse".

Consider the 24 Ss as a general guide for raising your child.

The 24 Ss reflect the frequent needs of children who have experienced abuse, neglect and multiple losses. They were developed by me over the years, in close collaboration with many foster carers and adoptive parents and associated professionals who were struggling to raise these children successfully. The first 16 are to be increased, and the final eight are to be decreased.

INCREASE

I. Safety

Your child – and you, for that matter – needs to feel safe if she is to manage well in any and, if possible, all areas of functioning. However, she often does not feel safe because of how her history has affected her perceptions, thoughts, feelings and associations with many of the objects and events of her life. When she hears your voice or looks into your eyes she is likely to hear rage and see hatred when you are only mildly annoyed. She will also not feel safe with changes, surprises or excitement. She needs information about what is happening or about to happen so that she has a chance to work through any emerging fears, and she may need assistance in making sense of it all. Consequences that involve isolation, emotional withdrawal, a harsh and punitive tone, or which might easily be seen as severe and rejecting will undermine safety and are very unlikely to be successful in the long run. Ensuring that your child can enjoy regular safe activities in your home, both with you and alone, that are unconditional – i.e. she does not have to earn them – will assist her in gradually coming to anticipate safety, not threats.

2. Success
Your child, as do all children (and adults), functions best when she is successful rather than when she experiences routine failure. Children with trauma and attachment difficulties tend to have too few experiences of success. There are at least two reasons for this:

a.   They are often burdened by expectations based on their chronological age rather than their overall developmental age. They are often not developmentally mature enough to manage the requirements for independent goal-directed behaviours, impulse control, delay of gratification, anticipation of consequences and self-regulation of their thoughts and feelings. The fact that they were able to do something "last Tuesday" does not mean that they are able to do it when they are under stress of any sort. (I may have been able to stay with my diet "last Tuesday" but not today.)

b.   They have difficulty learning from their mistakes, so they tend to make the same mistake over and over again. This is likely to relate to their perception that they did not make a mistake in the first place. They deny what happened, or minimise it, give an excuse or blame someone else. These are defences against shame and these children are likely to experience a pervasive sense of shame. Until their shame is greatly reduced, they will have serious difficulty in facing their "problems" and being open to alternative ways of thinking about, and perceiving their behaviours and associated events.

3. Structure

Your child will probably need more structure than other children of her chronological age. Free time is likely to cause anxiety; choices are likely to cause indecision and anxiety. However, it is crucial that when you provide structure, it is done in a spirit of giving her a gift, not as giving her a punishment. She needs structure in order to feel safe, in much the same way as younger children do. The structure provided should not be a series of chores or responsibilities, but rather a range of activities that meet her overall developmental needs, which involve being both active and quiet, interactive and solitary, and encourage her physical, cognitive, social and emotional areas of functioning.

4. Supervision

Your presence will offer your child a background sense of safety. Your presence helps her to inhibit her impulses and provides her with a sense of containment that she cannot achieve when alone. Your presence also helps her to know that you notice her and think of her. Until she develops a sense of attachment security with you, she is likely to experience separation as being "out of sight means out of mind". She is terrified that you will forget her (although she will not admit it to you). As with structure, your presence must be communicated as being a gift, not a punishment. Over time, she will hopefully begin to experience it in that way.

5. Soothing

When your child is able to accept soothing from you, she will have taken a big step toward learning to manage frustrations and fears without having to resort to anger or withdrawal. Many children with a history of abuse and neglect have extreme difficulty seeking – or even accepting when they are offered – comfort and cuddles if they are having a hard time. They sought to be soothed by their birth parents when they were very young and their efforts led to failure and increased pain and distress. So they stopped trying; they learnt to manage on their own.

Helping your child to accept soothing is a slow, gentle, patient process. If she will not accept a cuddle, lightly touch her hand or arm instead. If she will not accept any touch, comfort with your voice and eyes and quiet presence. If she will not accept your presence, give her a note or send her an email, bake her a treat, or leave a vase of flowers in her room. Be persistent, quietly and gently if necessary, but do not give up. If she can come to accept comforting, she will one day believe that she is worthy of being comforted.

6. Soup

Food is central to life and being provided with food by your parents is a basic message that you will always be cared for, no matter what. Your child may have gone hungry for days, she may have been punished by having her meal removed, she may have been screamed at while she ate. When she can accept your food and when she can enjoy a family dinner together, she will have taken a big step towards being able to share family life and actually feeling that she is a member of the family.

One adoptive mother told me that if she could tell when her daughter got out of bed in the morning that she was going to have a bad day, she prepared soup for dinner that evening for the family. She said that soup seemed to comfort her daughter and led her to feeling content, better than any other food. I know what she means; it has that effect on me as well.

7. Storytelling

By storytelling, I am primarily referring to trying to maintain a "storytelling" voice. This refers to a voice that is modulated, with rhythms, inflections, pauses and varying degrees of intensity. Such a voice holds your child's interest and helps her to feel that she is not being judged, but that you are engaged in describing events and experiences. The monotone voice is the opposite of storytelling and conveys a lecture, with judgment and often with disappointment or anger.

Storytelling can recall a stressful event as a story, by simply describing the sequence of what happened, including how you and your child experienced it, without making judgments. When you recount an enjoyable or stressful event you have shared with your child to your partner or other family member or friend in the same way, your child will listen intently to measure your interest in her and your appreciation of your time together. She is then likely to remember the event more clearly, with a greater sense of closeness to you.

Finally, when you literally tell your child a bedtime story each night, you will often find that she feels closer to you at the end of the day and falls asleep more easily. If she asks you to repeat the story the next night, you are onto something that you might want to cultivate. Try to tell a story every night, regardless of any conflicts you had with your child during the day.

8. Seeking meaning

When you and your child understand the meaning of her behaviour, both you and she are more likely to know what – if anything – you might do to change the behaviour if it is making her life or the lives of others more difficult. When your child develops the habit of knowing why she does things, she will become more empowered to handle her own behaviours. When she develops the habit of understanding why you do things as well, she is likely to be more able to understand and accept your limits and consequences.

9. Special

Your child needs to know that she is special-to-you. She is your child and that makes her unique and separates her from every child who is not your child. In being special-to-you, she will know that you have discovered what is unique about her. She will know that you accept all of her and that whatever you discover about her, she will always remain special-to-you.

10. Smiles

This refers to the goal of trying to maintain a positive attitude in the family. Even when intense conflicts with your child make it hard to be positive in moment-to-moment interactions with her, if you can protect the emotional atmosphere of the rest of the family, eventually your child with the challenging behaviours is likely to change her negative attitude so that it is more like the family's overall positive view of life. Without maintaining this positive attitude, there is a danger that the whole family may begin to reflect the negative attitude of your child.

11. Sense of humour

As was said earlier regarding playfulness, a sense of humour is very protective for both you and your child. Humour helps you to see the big picture, apart from the here-and-now challenges. It helps both you and your child to take conflicts less personally. Humour is often present when a relationship is being repaired and when the hard times of yesterday are being recalled. It helps to provide a context for the problems that are being faced.

12. Stretching

Stretching refers to being open and flexible enough to modify your child-rearing beliefs and practices to meet the unique, individual needs of your child. Maybe the way you were raised by your parents was good enough for you and you "turned out all right". Maybe the way you raised your other children was fine and they are doing well. However, a child who was abused and neglected by her birth parents, and then lost a series of caregivers through multiple moves, may well need a very specialised way of parenting.

13. Sorry

Saying that you are sorry to your child when you have done something that you regret or believe was a mistake, is crucial if you are to sustain your relationship with her. You do not lose authority when you say that you are sorry. Rather, your child will have greater respect for you for being able to admit that you made a mistake. You are also communicating that she is important enough to you to do something that is difficult for you, in order to make it right with her. Finally, saying that you are sorry is excellent modelling for her, as this is something that is likely to be very hard for her to do because of her pervasive sense of shame.

14. Sensory integration

During infancy, when your child's attachment organisation was developing along with her emotional, social, and cognitive abilities, her sensory-motor skills were also developing together with the crucial ability to be able to integrate these skills. If a child's development is compromised during infancy due to abuse, neglect, and loss, her specific sensory integration abilities were most likely compromised as well. This might contribute to her general difficulty in regulating her emotions, paying attention and behaviour. It might also contribute to difficulties with physical pressure and touch, movements, balance and co-ordination.

Many children would benefit from an assessment by a sensory integration specialist to determine if there are specific deficits that might well respond to activities you could engage in at home. I have noticed that at times, when a child demonstrates an improvement in her sensory integration abilities, there is a parallel improvement in her emotional regulation, attention span and concentration, and overall relationship skills.

15. Sleep

Your child might have significant difficulty in falling asleep or remaining asleep throughout the night. This may relate to many factors, including being traumatised or isolated in her bedroom, fear of the dark, nightmares, fear of loss of control or of abandonment, difficulty in making transitions, or her mind wandering into frightening scenarios before falling asleep.

It is very important to try to establish a bedtime routine that facilitates sleep. This routine needs to be individualised for your unique child. Once you find something that works, protect it and try not to vary it. Sometimes I think that a child's place in a new home is greatly enhanced or damaged depending on whether or not a successful sleep routine is established early in her new placement. One of the first questions a new adoptive parent might ask of the previous caregiver is when this child went to bed, the layout of the bedroom, and what activities were involved in the bedtime routine.

16. Self-care

It is crucial for a parent who is caring for a child who does not respond consistently or positively to the parent's initiatives to take care of herself. When a parent does not feel successful in her parenting goals – something that is likely to be a top priority in her life – the stress is likely to become intense. This places the parent at risk of having trouble regulating her own emotions, whereby anger becomes rage, fear becomes traumatic and sadness becomes despair. This parent is in danger of entering a state of shame over her inability to help her child to have a better life. Her brain might tell her that it is not her fault, but her heart tells her that this is her child and she needs to find something that will work. It is her responsibility and she is failing.

The open and engaged state previously described in this book works best when it meets a similar state within the other person involved, whether it be a partner, friend, or child. The neurological systems in the brain that are active in successful parenting are designed to work best when they are having an effect on the child – when the activity is reciprocal. Parenting may often be hard work, but it is much easier to parent for a long period of time when the acts of parenting seem to be making a difference – when your child is responding, learning, feeling your love and thriving within your care.

Central to taking care of self for a parent is to have some adult – a partner, relative, friend or empathic and understanding professional – to whom they can turn for comfort and support, understanding and empathy. This person must not judge you: must not judge your motives, innermost thoughts, feelings or wishes. If you whisper and cry with shame and say that you wish that you had never brought this child into your home, you must know that you will not be judged. You need a person who will relate to you with PACE, who will care for you in the way you have been trying to care for your child. If you are to continue caring for your child, you need to have someone important to you, caring for you.

In caring for yourself you need to care for your relationship with your partner. You need to remain a team, supporting and relieving each other if you are to parent your child who is rejecting you. Your child may deliberately try to cause conflict between you and your partner. You must protect this relationship.

And you need moments of peace, satisfaction, success, and pleasure. This may involve music, gardening, yoga, spirituality, reading, knitting or playing cards. But you need these moments. If you do not care for yourself consistently, you will have great difficulty consistently caring for your child who rejects you.

DECREASE

1. Shame

This has been explored above. Decreasing shame remains central in any efforts to help your child to reduce the impact of her traumatic history on her current functioning. She may hide her sense of shame behind a tough or indifferent pose. But have no doubt, she feels at her core that she is worthless, bad, and/or unlovable. When she begins to move away from these views of herself, she will begin to be open to your views of her and to learn how to live the life that you are offering her.

2. Stimulation

Your child is likely to be very easily over-stimulated by unexpected or mildly exciting events. This will cause immediate dysregulation of her emotional, cognitive, and behavioural functioning. What started out as a celebration, outing, family reunion, or reward for a job well done might well have ended as another ruined activity with much anger and frustration for all involved, including your child. She was not able to regulate her positive emotion that was generated by the event.

It is crucial that you learn what amount of stimulation and what types of activities your child can manage and for how long. You need to learn what assistance she may need to get her through an event. You need to learn if she has to skip certain events or activities and to be provided with alternatives that have a degree of stimulation that she can manage. You need to be an advocate for your child, letting well-meaning others know that while they want to give your child an enjoyable experience or reward her good behaviour, the treat they are providing will only end in failure. Most "rewards" are not objectively rewarding. They may actually be failures and sources of distress when they do not match your child's ability to regulate and integrate them.

3. Shouting

When you were young – and I was young – it is likely that your parents, and mine, disciplined us with a tone of voice that was stern and conveyed a mild to moderate degree of annoyance. That tone got our attention and made us aware that we needed to change our behaviour in the direction indicated or there would be a more significant consequence. Your child may not respond to such routine sternness, and you may find yourself increasing the intensity of your tone and becoming more annoyed. You may also find that you are becoming more and more angry because your child's behaviours are more and more disruptive and defiant. You may find yourself shouting for much of the day, with little effect on your child's behaviour. But the atmosphere of your home has become negative, you and other family members are more tense, irritable, or withdrawn. And you have a headache.

Since routine discipline and the associated stern lecture is not effective, you might do better by trying to routinely use PACE to discipline your child, rather than anger. This is easier said than done, but becomes easier if you notice that your child eventually starts to respond a bit better to PACE. Being sad for her over the consequences of her actions rather than mad at her for her actions tends to help the child to focus more on her behaviour and to be more interested in knowing why she acted that way, than if she became defensive and felt more shame in response to your anger. It helps her to see that your discipline relates to her behaviour, not to herself and not to her relationship with you.

This is not to suggest that you should never be angry. As I said before, you are not a robot. You have "bad hair days". Accept it, own it, and don't blame your child for it. But let her know that you have less patience on that day and you might be a bit grumpy. Your child may give you some space on that day because you are not blaming her for it. You are not perfect, just as she is not perfect.

Also, if this grumpiness is the worst behaviour that your child will experience from you – and you have not abused, neglected or abandoned her – she is likely to feel more safe rather than less safe after such days.

Finally, sometimes being angry when your child does something that seems outrageous may be necessary and the most appropriate response. If she kicks the dog, she may need to see that you are angry about that behaviour in order to appreciate how serious it was. If you save your anger for such major incidents, not routine misbehaviour, she is likely to benefit from it in those instances. And if you repair your relationship as soon as possible after the expression of anger, she is likely to feel guilt over her behaviour, rather than shame.

4. Seclusion

Isolation in response to misbehaviour is likely to reduce your child's sense of safety. She needs your presence in order to have a chance to regulate her emotions. She needs to know that she will not be rejected or abandoned. During her years of abuse and neglect, she was probably isolated on many occasions. You would not isolate your child when she is afraid or sad, so why isolate her when she is angry? Stay near her – not to give her a lecture or to "process" what she did wrong, but simply to give her your presence to calm her, to reduce her shame, and to help her be receptive to your guidance so she can get back on her feet again. It is usually wise not to start a dialogue or stare at her when she is still upset. Just be nearby so that she can see you are regulated and available for her. When she is ready, you will be there for her in whatever way she needs you to be.

5. Should

This refers to raising the child based on her chronological age rather than on her developmental age. When you or another adult starts to speak about your child by saying: 'She should be able to do that, she's eight years old...,' it is likely that the expectations are not matched to your child's abilities. You need to know your child and forget the word "should". Besides, about half of the suggestions you will get are that you are "too hard" and the other half will say that you are "too easy".

6. Sarcasm

As parents work to shout less, the danger is that they will become more sarcastic. If it is a choice between the two, shouting is probably easier than sarcasm for the child to manage. With shouting, it is clearer that you are angry and why you are angry. With sarcasm, your child often knows that something is wrong regarding her behaviour and/or her relationship with you, but she will be more anxious about it as she may find it harder to understand what is wrong.

7. Smacking

In general, physical discipline is likely to have more negative consequences than positive ones with regard to your child's behaviour, her self-concept, and your relationship with her. However, when physical discipline is used on a child who has experienced abuse and neglect in the past, it will have far greater negative effects. It will increase your child's sense of shame and lack of safety, and so reverse the positive development of your relationship.

8. Secrets

Keeping secrets from your child about matters that relate to her can prevent her developing a sense of safety and make her less able to trust you now and in the future. She needs to know her history, even those parts that happened long before her mind would be able to consciously remember them. She needs to know why and how decisions and plans were made for her. She needs to know when adults made mistakes. Such knowledge may, in the short term, create more anxiety and disruptive behaviour, but in

48

the long term it will give her a foundation of truth upon which to develop a secure base.

This does not mean that she should be told everything now. It means that when we discuss information that relates to the child, we do not discuss "if" she is to be told but rather "when", "how" and "by whom". We also consider what is in place to support your child when she may be struggling to integrate the new knowledge.

CHAPTER **5**

How the child might be affected at different stages of development

All children will experience some stress, uncertainty and confusing thoughts, feelings, and wishes as they move from one developmental milestone to the next. For all children, the increasing time spent at school, along with the more complex academic and social expectations, create a new series of challenges from year to year. As the years go on, your child will be expected to work more independently, delay gratifications, show greater impulse control, communicate more verbally, and work towards increasingly long-term goals. To be successful he will need to develop greater emotional regulation, improved attention span and concentration, greater tolerance of frustration, and improved problem-solving skills.

Children who have been abused, neglected and experienced loss are likely to show early delays in their social, emotional, cognitive, behavioural and general regulation skills. Often these early delays make new learning difficult so that the gap between them and their peers increases from year to year. As your child becomes more "different" from his peers, and these differences become more noticed by him, the stress involved with functioning well at school and with his peers can become more and more intense.

Children with troubled histories are also more vulnerable than other children to being hypersensitive and hyper-reactive to routine stresses. This means that your child may be likely to perceive others as rejecting him or making fun of him when that was not the intention of the teacher or other child involved. He may have trouble "using his words", because he has not developed his ability to find the words that might express aspects of his inner life. Such children would probably benefit from a very individualised educational approach, but often do not receive it because they are thought not to be trying hard enough, or as being too sensitive or too quick to "fly off the handle". It is easy to think that if they just tried harder they would not have any problems.

Your child will also be vulnerable as he moves into adolescence. Sexual feelings and expectations from peers may trigger traumatic experiences associated with past sexual abuse. Peer pressure and general societal expectations to be more independent from their parents often activate a strong desire in adolescents for greater freedom and independence when they are not yet ready to manage the associated responsibilities. They, and others, think that they "should" be more independent so they pull away from their parents. But their parents know that they are not ready for that degree of independence, which can often create intense parent–child conflict.

Adolescence also produces an increase in reflective functioning. Your child with a troubled history is likely to find his mind going back to the past, trying to understand it or trying to undo it. He may hold on to an unrealistic view of his birth parents, thinking that if he could reunite with them again, all would go well this time, and any current unhappiness would disappear. If he has not been given help over the years to make sense of and resolve early traumatic experiences, the memory of them may lead him into self-destructive behaviour.

CHAPTER 6

Education and social issues

A good school performance is difficult to attain consistently when the mental abilities of exploration and learning tend not to have a high priority because a child – or adult – does not feel safe. If they have not established a secure base of safety within their home, children often do not feel safe enough to manage the stresses of daily activities within school and with their peers. There is much research that indicates that attachment security facilitates the desire to learn and the cognitive focus required to learn well.

There are other reasons why your child might not do well in school, some of which are listed here.

- There is too much stimulation.

- She is asked to work independently to a greater extent than she is capable of.

- She does not have a meaningful relationship to enable consequences to be effective.

- She does not have an adult present whom she identifies as an attachment figure.

- There are too many adults involved in meeting her educational needs.

- She has difficulty managing her emotions and behaviour and this interferes with her ability to focus on her schoolwork.

- Her frequent misbehaviour evokes angry responses from her teachers and she experiences this anger as being rejecting and shameful, which interferes with her motivation to learn and co-operate.

- She is chronically defensive, rather than open and engaged with others.

Louise Bomber (2007, 2011) has written two excellent books to assist teachers in developing educational programmes that better meet the developmental needs of these children.

Conclusion

In summary, I hope that I have stressed adequately the often pervasive, long-term effects of abuse, neglect and attachment losses and betrayals on your child's overall development and day-to-day functioning, and on how these effects can cause emotional and behavioural difficulties. Since these effects may be less obvious on certain days or in particular settings, we tend to forget that they are still present, ready to emerge under conditions of stress, uncertainty or change. The very process of your child beginning to trust you and believing that you love him may create anxiety and lead to increased emotional and behavioural problems.

The horrible fact that your child did experience maltreatment does not excuse his current misbehaviour. However, that maltreatment is most likely a central reason for his misbehaviour. While he is still accountable to behave in more appropriate ways, he deserves our understanding that the reasons from his past are very hard for him to overcome – that his life as a child is likely to be much harder than our lives have ever been. He also deserves that we work hard to understand the specific experiences and memories that continue to haunt him so that we can provide him with the safety, structure, supervision and support needed to assist him in being successful.

I have written a small book of poems in an effort to capture the experience of children who have experienced trauma and loss, as well as their journey towards hope and trust in their new families (Hughes, 2012). This book concludes with one of them.

Your sweet persistence
When you brought me to your house
from the empty lands,
I hoped for days with
food, clothes,
not much work,
not too hot, not too cold.
and nights without fear, pain or touch.

It never occurred to me to want more,
I did not know that there was more.
It was months before I knew enough to know
the real meaning of the empty lands,
and the memory of them became even more painful –
I discovered the pain of discovering what had been missing.

Not knowing love
I was terrified of your love –
thinking that I would no longer exist
if I accepted it.
And then when – not if –
you took it away
I would be nothing.

It was your gentle presence –
your sweet persistence –

in touching me with your smile and voice
and teaching me that these touches were called
comfort, care, compassion, companionship.

It was your loud laugh –
your merry eyes –
that led me from safety to happiness
to rising ripples of joy
that carried me home
and hurled me up among the stars.

So now as I reflect on my life
in the empty lands
I feel sadness for my unseen self
but not fear or shame.
You – my parents –
finding me and loving me –
fill me with gratitude,
with comfort, and with joy.

SECTION 1

PARENTING CHILDREN AFFECTED BY EMOTIONAL AND BEHAVIOURAL DIFFICULTIES

LORNA MILES

JESS AND PAUL GETHIN

How it feels

Lorna Miles

I have never been a fan of fairgrounds and theme parks – in fact, the exact opposite could be said because as soon as I know that we are going to visit one I start to panic. My stomach turns somersaults, my heart rate increases and visions of all kinds of scenarios that could lead to injury or worse flash through my mind. For me to have a reaction as extreme as this, you would assume that I have been involved in, or witnessed, some kind of horrific accident, but you would be wrong.

This reaction, which is out of all proportion to the situation, has resulted from my mother's anxieties and her determination that, for whatever reason, her children would not engage in an activity which was, in her opinion, potentially life-threatening. Of course, as an adult I have been able to see that her fears are totally unfounded: after all, how many theme park accidents do we hear about? What about the strict health and safety legislation? I am able to talk myself through the reality of the situation and allow the children in my care, and on occasion myself, to enjoy "all the fun of the fair".

We all experience situations we find difficult; we may dread having to do certain things or to meet people who, for some inexplicable reason, we just can't take to – perhaps we actively avoid them, feel incredibly irritated by them or find ourselves reacting in a way that is totally out of character. More often than not, once we explore these feelings we discover that the reasons for them are rooted in our own attachment histories. Our life experiences may have impacted on and magnified the issue and, in some cases, can have serious implications for our day-to-day living. Of course, trips to theme parks are planned events and to some extent we can plan how to deal with the situation or even avoid it completely. But what about those triggers which are involuntary, or set off by others, perhaps by a comment or attitude, by body language or the environment in which the exchange takes place?

Triggers

Whilst working as a social work assistant, I had to facilitate contact between a child and her grandparents. The grandfather had a military background and appearances were important for him. He would comment on muddy shoes, unkempt hair and general appearance; he never showed any signs of affection for his granddaughter. Instead of helping the child to deal with this, I found myself worrying about my own appearance: a sense of panic in my chest, shoes hastily rubbed on the leg of my trousers, coat or cardigan neatly buttoned up, a quick pat of the head to make sure my hair was in place. It was several weeks before I was even aware that I was doing this – all I knew was that I dreaded the sessions and found them exhausting.

One evening as I was driving home, having just taken the child back to her carers, a sudden thought came to me. Shoes: that was it, shoes! It was the grandfather's preoccupation with clean shoes that was arousing my feelings of anxiety. I grew up living next door to my paternal grandparents; my father worked for them in the family business and was paid a very small wage, in relation to the hours he worked and the responsibility he held. In my grandmother's view, my mother over-indulged her daughters where shoes were concerned: one pair a year would have been sufficient, and new shoes for each school term was, in her view, a luxury my father could ill afford. New shoes had to be hidden from my grandmother's eagle eye: they would be worn to school but then we hastily changed back into our old shoes, which my grandmother would check for wear and tear. A reprimand was issued if we were not taking sufficient care of them. 'Your poor father, how do you think he can afford to buy you girls new shoes on the wage he earns? Go and put some polish on those shoes now!'

Once I had made the connection between the feelings I was experiencing in the present and the anxieties coming from my past, I was able to engage my "adult" brain and manage the sessions in a much more appropriate way. As the contact only took a couple of hours each time it wasn't a major issue in my life, but what if these feelings are triggered by a child in your care and with whom you live 24/7?

Mike

Mike, when he came to us at the age of nine, had the attitude and "swagger" you would expect from a streetwise teenager. As a female in his world, I clearly deserved to be treated as a second-class citizen, whose views counted for nothing. Everything I said was dismissed and he tried his best to make me feel intimidated and "small". Many of his behaviours were confrontational and challenging, which created a tense family atmosphere.

We had been therapeutic foster carers for some time, trained and experienced in using Dan Hughes' methods, and dealing with challenging behaviour was nothing new, but something was making me feel impotent; I wasn't frightened of Mike, but he was stirring up feelings I didn't understand and, if I am honest, I didn't really find him likeable.

Tim, my husband, could see that I was struggling and couldn't make sense of it either – what was going on here? Slowly I began to notice that many of the demeaning comments Mike directed to me were not made when Tim was around; in fact, although still very "upfront" in his behaviour regardless of who was in the house, Mike showed two very different sides of himself, and the one that appeared when I was on my own with him was the one which was causing the problem.

My initial introduction to parenting with PACE had been reading the work of Dan Hughes. His observation that a child will "drive a battleship" between spouses or partners if mutual communication is not a high priority had, in our experience, been very true. If you are not aware of this you can quickly fall into the trap of allowing the child to recreate an atmosphere of turmoil and conflict, which has often been the norm for him or her and one in which they feel more comfortable. Because Tim and I were able to talk about the situation openly and honestly, we could unravel how Mike's dismissive attitude and apparent lack of interest in anything I had to say was recreating my experience as a teenager, when I felt that within my family my views were worthless – what my father said was final, there was no discussion.

Once I realised this, things started to improve; Mike's attitude didn't change but I was able to respond in a more playful way and not take Mike's attitude towards me personally. He wasn't with us long enough for us to make a big difference to his life, but by the time he left, I was able to describe him as a likeable lad.

Levi and Dwain

As I look back over our fostering experiences since the early 1980s, I am struck by how certain children have triggered responses I wouldn't have expected. After being a foster carer for a few years you can feel like you have "been there, done it and got the T-shirt", as the saying goes. But you can be caught off guard, and in my experience it is the specific presentation of the child that is the trigger for how you respond.

Levi and Dwain, aged six and nine years respectively, were placed with us on a voluntary basis for a two-week period, whilst their mother, Diane, gave evidence in a drugs-related court case. They arrived for their two-week stay with barely enough clothes for a weekend, let alone two weeks. Their social worker had suggested that they brought some familiar toys and possessions with them, but they arrived with only a very small backpack each, clothes escaping because the zips were broken. Despite having had a "bit of an accident" en-route and needing to be changed, Levi had a broad grin on his face; he had big blue eyes that seemed to be full of joy. Dwain, on the other hand, had a dark, sullen look and despite being only nine years old, had deep frown lines across his forehead. He stood tall and upright, shoulders back, and surveyed his surroundings with a look of disdain.

Levi quickly spotted our cat lounging on the chair and moved off to play with him, Dwain just plonked himself on the sofa glaring at everyone. The social worker completed the paperwork and went on her way. When Tim and I took the boys to see their rooms Levi delighted in the toys we had provided and immediately selected some to play with, but Dwain threw his bag on the bed and stomped off downstairs.

By lunchtime we had provided Levi with several dry pairs of pants and trousers from our "spares" as wherever he went a trail of urine was left behind. He was oblivious and played merrily whilst Dwain looked on in disgust. Eventually, by mid-afternoon, Dwain could contain himself no longer. 'It's you own bloody fault, why haven't you given him the potty?' I assumed that he meant the potty that toddlers use for toilet training, but Levi was six years old – surely not! Before I could respond Dwain had marched off to the bathroom and returned with a potty in his hand. He proceeded to take Levi's trousers and pants off and gave him the receptacle to hold. Levi placed it between his legs and sat down; wherever he went the potty went too. He walked along holding it between his legs and became very distressed if I tried to part him from it. Periodically Dwain would march Levi off to the bathroom where the potty was emptied and returned, it was even put on the chair to boost Levi to table height at mealtimes and prevented him from piddling on the chair.

The court case took many twists and turns and Diane's mental health went into decline. The boys' stay, which happened to be during the school summer holidays, was extended, and Dwain's observations of my "mistakes" increased. As the stay went on, I, surprisingly, once again began to doubt my ability to be a parent.

I knew that children in the past had triggered responses linked to my own history, but I had dealt with that, hadn't I? Yet now each day was starting to fill me with dread – what would I do wrong today? Tim was getting a little impatient with my constant need for reassurance: 'For goodness sake, you've brought up David and Malcolm and cared for lots of other children. Why are you letting this get to you?' I didn't know.

Adopting David and Malcolm after years of infertility had been a difficult decision for me, it meant that I had to accept that I couldn't produce a child of our own made out of the love Tim and I shared. I looked at women around me, many of whom hadn't even planned a pregnancy, wandering around with their "bumps" and felt like a failure. Well-meaning relatives gave me birthday gifts of seductive nightwear and expensive wines, hinting that '...it might do the trick.' Instead, it only served to increase my feelings of inadequacy. My paternal grandfather suggested I should accept that I wasn't going to be a mother, because clearly if I had been "up to the job" children would have naturally come along.

I assumed that it was Dwain's surly attitude that was causing the difficulty at the time and it was long after Levi and Dwain had returned home with a programme of support in place, that I started to make links between Dwain's behaviour and the hurtful comments made many years ago. His stance, body language, tone of voice and overall attitude were very similar to those of my grandfather.

Unexpected feelings

Other adopters and foster carers, particularly those who have taken older children, have spoken to me about the unexpected feelings triggered by their child's attitude, behaviours or mannerisms.

Of course, recognising and understanding our attachment patterns is one thing, reorganising them and responding in different ways is another and won't happen overnight. Even with the help of counselling or therapy, it takes time to explore the past and reflect on why we are reacting in a particular way. That can be tough when a child is reinforcing how you are feeling; children with attachment issues are masters at finding your weak spots and gnawing away at them incessantly. Finding the right person to "hold you" whilst you make this often painful journey can be a problem too. If your partner is embroiled in a triangle of conflict that the child is creating, they might not be able to help, and my own personal experience is that family and friends just don't "get it": they can sympathise if you are dealing with difficult, challenging behaviour, they may even show empathy, '…know how you feel…' or ask 'Why do you put up with it?' but the powerful way in which traumatised children can invade your psyche and turn you into someone that even you yourself can't recognise, has to be experienced to be understood.

Lying and stealing

Although at times we struggle to understand why certain behaviours are difficult to manage or why they "press buttons" that make it hard to control our own emotions, there are other behaviours we find difficult to deal with because they go against the values that form part of our own moral framework and that of society in general. Lying and stealing fall into this category and phrases like 'I just can't stand it when he/she lies' or 'Why he/she doesn't just admit they did it...' can often be heard when foster carers and adopters get together. Habitual lying and stealing, backed up by stories so outrageous that no one on earth would ever believe them, or denial that leaves you doubting what you know to be true, seem commonplace amongst the population of children who have been touched by the care system. But why and how do we deal with it?

Charlie

'Just leave the bags alone until Tim has finished unloading the car, they need to go on the kitchen unit not in the living room....Thank you!' Tim had kindly stopped off on the way home from work to do the weekly supermarket shop, and as soon as he opened the front door Charlie, aged ten, appeared in the hallway, snatched the bags from his hands and started tipping them out onto the sofa. The dogs thought their birthdays and Christmases had been rolled into one as packs of meat, cheese and other delicious goodies fell on the floor and were hastily whisked off for immediate consumption.

'Charlie, please put everything in the kitchen...no I don't know when we are having the sausages but it will be one night next week...Some of the sweets are yours but not all of them...yes, the biscuits too...'

Charlie's ample waistline was a clear indicator of his eating habits, but no one seemed to appreciate just what a difficult relationship with food he had or the lengths he would go to get it. I frequently found food he had stashed away in his room, cheese, crisps, or a packet of ham. But he claimed he had no idea how they had got there. Even when he was caught with pockets bulging with goodies he feigned complete surprise and disbelief at their presence.

I could no longer trust him to go to the village shops alone as despite knowing us well and being sympathetic about the problems our foster children faced, the local shop owners were losing patience with the fact that fifty pence worth of sweets in a bag were accompanied by a pound's worth of sweets in Charlie's pockets.

Food wasn't really restricted in our house and we had learned long ago that trying to change children's eating habits within days of arrival just didn't work, but Charlie was proving to be something of a challenge. Stealing food was bad enough, but lying about it was even worse. The problem wasn't confined to home: his school suspected that he was responsible for taking food that was disappearing from other children's lunch boxes and he was quick to take and eat the food other children left from their school dinners.

One of the issues when dealing with problems of this kind is that we tend to look at them from our own moral perspective – stealing and lying are wrong and that is all there is to it. Most of us can't envisage a world where this might be different; our own moral code has been shaped by our experience of life. Our parents corrected us when we did things that were not socially acceptable and we learned right from wrong.

One of the 24 Ss that Dan Hughes refers to earlier in this book is 'Seeking the meaning of the behaviour'; this process can often be helped by looking at the "paperwork" for the child or talking to their social worker, to gain an understanding of the child's life story.

We have found the following questions useful to help us to understand what is going on.

1. What do we know about the child's past, that may explain the behaviour and be their motivator?

2. Have they been "taught" to behave in this way and believe it to be normal?

3. Could maintaining the behaviour be an important way to stay loyal to their family?

4. Is the "story" we are being told completely fictitious or could elements of it be true, with bits added to make it more acceptable?

5. Has the child rehearsed the story in their mind so often that they believe it is true?

6. What consequence might they fear if we find out the truth?

7. Are they using the behaviour to confirm feelings of worthlessness or a core belief – "I am bad"?

8. Are they using the behaviour to create an atmosphere in the house they are familiar with? Predictable negative responses from adults can be better than unpredictable positive ones. A turbulent environment can feel familiar and safer than an unfamiliar calm atmosphere.

9. Are they using the behaviour to get back at the world?

10. Are our own responses and reactions feeding the situation?

Like many children who are in care, Charlie's world had been about survival. His mum's drug and alcohol problems resulted in there often not being any food to eat. It had become Charlie's role to ensure that the family had food on the table, and he was rewarded by his mum with sweets when his forays were successful. Sweets became a safety net and currency for Charlie. If he couldn't steal something from a lunchbox, most of the children at his school who had packed lunches were willing to swap a sandwich for sweets, and if later in the day Charlie discovered that the cupboards at home were bare, the sandwich was better than nothing. Perhaps a sandwich could be used to appease an angry parent? If Charlie had sweets he was safe. Also associated with rewards, they had become a symbol of success and a sweet in his mouth allowed him to have a rare moment when he felt good about himself.

What seemed like ridiculous food to hoard in a bedroom – cheese, ham and other items – were literally survival rations for Charlie. He had no idea about "sell by dates", refrigeration and the like, he just knew that there could be times when he wouldn't be able to steal enough food for the day or that what he did steal would be eaten by one of his "dads" and he needed to know that he had something in reserve.

Eating the other children's "leftovers" at school, even though he wasn't hungry, was another way of making sure he had enough to eat that day, in case nothing was available later. He was eating far more than was healthy for him in his quest not to feel hungry, for being hungry reminded him of his difficult circumstances.

Charlie knew that his family wasn't like most of his friends' families, and so lying about the reality seemed like the only option to him. Like the lies he needed to tell his mum, or the men in her life, if he returned home with no food. Perhaps lies were the only defence available to protect himself from abusive punishment, ridicule and humiliation, all of which confirmed that he was "bad". Lies were needed for self-preservation and, like stealing, had become a part of Charlie's behaviour in order for him to survive.

The motivation behind Charlie's behaviour was not unusual; we have cared for children who have spoken about stealing newspapers from letterboxes, hubcaps and other automobilia, money or electronic devices, and often selling them on the streets to buy food or even fund their parents' addictions. A mum on drugs can be safer to live with than one suffering from withdrawal symptoms. Again, it all boils down to self-preservation and results in the child developing a completely different moral compass from that of most people.

Some children declare that the world owes them in order to justify their actions. 'You owe me, I've had a tough life...' was the answer I received to my enquiry about why my credit card statement listed a number of expensive transactions relating to an online gaming site!

Of course, an angry adult response to lying or stealing can be predictable for the child, so in some bizarre way this also makes them feel safe: it's what they know, and so continuing the behaviour creates a kind of security.

In Charlie's case it was clear that much of what we were dealing with in the present was inextricably linked to the past; we needed to help him feel safe before we could make any progress. Charlie couldn't trust that there would always be food available in our house and that he wouldn't receive physical punishment. He needed concrete evidence and reminders that this was the case. We needed to make a shift too: it wasn't that Charlie didn't believe what we said to him, it was that he *couldn't* believe it, not yet.

A rummage in the kitchen cupboards with Charlie provided him with a box containing a "stash" of non-perishable food he could keep in his room in case there were days when there was no food. We had to respect the importance of this to him; I couldn't just dash upstairs and raid it for a tin of baked beans if I ran out.

A tub of sweets, which we kept topped up, provided him with the "currency" he needed to feel safe. He was consuming far more sweets than was good for him but we needed to focus on breaking his habit of stealing sweets, health promotion could come later!

We started to take a more laid back approach when food went missing. 'Hey Charlie, did you know that mice like orange creams, one got in the fridge last night and ate all the ones in the box of chocolates Tim gave me.'

Charlie didn't comment but a mutual understanding about the true course of events began to develop between us. Charlie wasn't being accused so he didn't need to defend himself by weaving a web of lies.

We verbalised why he might have been stealing food and acknowledged that, given the same circumstances, we would probably have done the same. He wasn't bad; he had been smart to find ways to survive.

We were clear with Charlie about what the consequence of taking things from outside our home would be, and continuously reminded him about the "stash" in his room. Any food found in the "stash" box, which shouldn't have been there, had to be "paid" for by doing little jobs around the home.

Television programmes and real-life situations provided opportunities to comment on the body language and signs that might indicate that someone is lying. 'Oh dear, you can tell that boy is lying because his face is going pink, do you think the teacher will notice?' Often children like Charlie have no idea that this is a possibility.

At first Charlie found this strategy incredibly difficult to deal with – we weren't responding in a way that was predictable and he felt out of control, but very slowly things started to change.

By the time Charlie left us to move on to a long-term placement, the stealing had stopped. He took his food "stash" with him. Who knows, he may still have it today as a safety net to make sure he never has to go hungry!

There have been many "Charlies" in our life over the

years and dealing with stealing and lying remains a challenge. One of the things I often think of when faced with this situation are the words of the psychologist Alfred Alder: '...A lie would have no sense unless the truth were felt as dangerous.' We have all told lies from time to time, and when I think about those times in my life, there has always been a link to a perceived safety within the lie. My boss won't sack me if I say I'm ill, but he might if I admit I've taken time off to go to my son's school play. Or: I'm saving my own embarrassment if the scratch has "mysteriously" appeared on my car rather than admitting I misjudged the distance when I wheeled the shopping trolley back to the trolley park! I try to remember this when a child is telling me something I am almost certain is not true,

I also ask myself what I hope to gain by making a child face fear, just for the satisfaction of proving that I am right. And there have been occasions when "stories" have seemed so outrageous that I have been convinced they have been lies, and it has later come to light that they were indeed true. Something that seems outrageous may have been normal in a child's world. Remembering not to use our own life experience to sort fact from fiction is important.

When new children join the family, is it better to prevent theft by securing our valuables and then relaxing as we get to know the child or to leave valuables exposed and then have to pick up the pieces when things go wrong? It might not feel right to lock things away in our own home, and it certainly isn't how most of us would choose to "parent", but is it a better option than setting the child up to fail, and reinforcing their belief that they are "bad?" The social stigma attached to lying and stealing makes it a difficult topic to discuss; people are quick to judge and children can be ostracised as a result. But is it better to warn family and friends about "light-fingered habits" the child may have, or to risk losing a friendship when something of theirs is taken?

Having used Dan Hughes' methods now for almost eight years, we have no doubts about their effectiveness in bringing about change in very troubled children. In fact, working in this way has become second nature, a way of life. However, this isn't without its challenges when children come into our care whose "team" aren't familiar with this way of working. We have also been fortunate enough to have had the support of our adult adopted children, and often wonder if we could work in this way if we had younger children of our own – what would the impact on their lives be?

Living and working in this way isn't easy, but remember, you can only do the best you can, stick to the principles of Dan's methods as far as possible and do what you think is right at the time. Often thinking "outside the box" and looking for the meaning behind the behaviour can be the key to moving forward.

One of the things I really enjoy about being a foster carer is the fact that no two days are the same, and you often don't know what behavioural challenges a child will bring for you to deal with. Every child I have cared for has uncovered strengths in me that I didn't know I had or enhanced those I was aware of, but they have also exposed or challenged my vulnerabilities, some of which may never have surfaced had we not chosen to live with these vulnerable and often damaged children.

SECTION II

I have learned the hard way that taking time for yourself is not a luxury but a necessity. Make time for your art group, yoga, worship or whatever you do for relaxation. Make time to re-connect with your partner and other family members and ask them to tell you if they think you are showing signs of stress. Spend some time exploring your past – preferably before things reach the crisis stage. You may decide to seek professional therapeutic help; this is never a sign of weakness but a positive step towards doing the best you can for the children in your care.

You have to have lived it

Jess and Paul Gethin

*We had always wanted a large family.
Six children had sounded good, but it was
not to be that easy, and five attempts
at IVF later, we were still childless. My
mother was adopted, and I had grown up
with an underlying desire to adopt and
so we embarked on our journey…*

Finding "our children" – the dream

We had only just been approved and our social worker,
Sue, had called round to offer her congratulations. To our
surprise, standing on our doorstep she paused, stared at
me intently, and almost in a whisper blurted out 'There
are three little ones…' My face must have lit up, for it
was what we so desperately wanted: a sibling group of
three, an instant family to love and cherish. My mind

was already sorting out beds and bedding when she tentatively continued with 'but their birth parents have learning difficulties, and the children are too young to say what the implications might be…'

Looking back, although we spoke to the medical adviser about genetic risks, met and listened to the foster carer, and repeatedly read the information we had been given about the children, there was never really any question that these weren't going to be "our children". They were so young at nearly two, three and four, and so impressionable that, despite knowing they had witnessed considerable violence and been terribly neglected, we were convinced they would thrive with us and be happy.

Getting to know the children – the reality sinks in
Sophie
The first day at our house was an eye-opener! Sophie, the eldest, appeared content in the garden with us and her siblings, but the minute we suggested going into the house, she threw herself down and kicked and screamed. We had looked forward to this day for so long, and I still remember our disappointment as all attempts to calm her failed. I scoured the backs of neighbouring houses to check for twitching curtains – the thought even crossed my mind that someone might phone the police, understandably concerned by the noise emanating from a house in which, prior to that moment, there had been no children. We quickly learnt that this was no ordinary "tantrum". It was screaming like her life depended on it – a deafening noise that could go on for hours at a time. But there was no consoling her, or getting close; there was no reasoning with her or snapping her out of it…it was both upsetting and exhausting.

What were we to do? On top of Sophie's experiences of neglect and violence in her birth family, her foster carer had clearly disliked her, at one point describing her to us as a "horrid child". We wanted her to understand that she was lovely and to show her love and affection – to make everything alright. But this was not how we had imagined it would be. We thought she would hug us, and we would hug her, but she was rigid and emotionless. It felt false and uncomfortable. Furthermore, when playing with us, she did not have the fun we had envisaged. She simply did not know how to play, or want to. All she wanted was to watch television, and the minute it was turned off, she had a tantrum.

Ben

At nearly three, Ben was still not talking and it was suggested that we learn sign language to communicate with him. He was clearly traumatised by events in his past, would cover his head at the sound of any loud noise and would storm off and hide when things did not go his way, or shriek in protest. Gradually, as we offered him lots of our time and unconditional love, speech came. Unfortunately, however, the effects of his early trauma on his emotions and behaviour were to be far more enduring.

Lucy

Little Lucy was a lively toddler whom everyone adored. She was most contented when playing with water and "cleaning"; in fact, she never tired of it. She struggled with speech, but smiled readily at everyone. It was later on that her liveliness was diagnosed as Attention Deficit Hyperactivity Disorder (ADHD), and her repetitive play as symptomatic of Autistic Spectrum Disorder. Unfortunately, it also became apparent that her ready

SECTION II

81

smile hid an inability to understand social behaviour; she would run into and push other children in an attempt to communicate, and failed to understand why they avoided her. A need to be in control of any play with other children further isolated her, and frequently she would sob that she was stupid and that nobody liked her.

Adjusting expectations

The first few years actually flew past and the children were unquestionably thriving. They glowed with health, and were increasingly affectionate towards us, and with each other. However, life as parents had certainly not been as we expected. Our children were definitely different from the norm.

A need for containment

The first time I took the children to a parent and toddler group, while the other children played with the toys, our three worked together using boxes, baskets – in fact, anything they could find – to collect up the toys scattered over the floor of the large hall. Not to play with them, but to pile them up under a blanket in a corner. This was to be repeated for many years with the toys that we gave them at home, which would be hidden in corners, under chairs and tables – out of reach for the play that was intended. They also searched for bags, and would regularly carry around supermarket bags stuffed full with clothes or toys.

At school, anything Lucy wrote or drew on paper was rapidly folded and put in a container with string or tape wound around it. When she started to lose her baby teeth they were wrapped in copious amounts of tissue and tied with string before being left under her pillow. The tooth fairy was nearly caught out on several occasions when Lucy attached the other end of the string to her finger!

The reasons for this behaviour no doubt had many causes, for example, the loss of the children's birth family, the neglect they had suffered, and being taught to steal and hide goods. But we also felt that their behaviour revealed a deep need to feel physically contained, and when there was not enough structure (such as during playtimes at school) they could not cope either emotionally or behaviourally.

Hyper-vigilance/need to be in control

Another characteristic of our children was their hyper-vigilance and need to be in control. Ben had to know about everything that was happening around him. In fact, it was virtually impossible to have a conversation in the house without him listening in. Unlike the other children, he would even avoid watching television if it meant being in a different room from us and not seeing and hearing what was going on.

Both the need to be in control and this hyper-vigilance were, we concluded, fear-based. Whilst Ben could appear like an angry, rude child who just wanted his own way, he was actually constantly stressed because his early experiences had taught him not to trust others and that he had to look out for himself. We learnt that it was invariably best to tell the children about what was going on and to avoid surprises. For example, if we were going out in a rush and didn't explain to Ben where and why we were going, and allow him time to adjust to what was happening, he would often shout at us and become aggressive. We recognised that he was not actually being naughty, but that we had not considered how stressful the sudden change in activity was for him. The answer was to give him lots of warning before we did anything, and plenty of positive reassuring information that made him feel special. If he needed a new coat, we would say, 'We are going to the shops in five minutes to get you a new coat because we want to make sure that if it gets cold, you will be kept warm, and we thought you might like to help choose the coat because you make really good choices'. Where we could, we let him feel that he was in control: if he helped to choose the coat, he would feel less threatened and be more co-operative.

Also, although we insisted that things such as bedtimes were controlled by us, so that the children felt safe and secure in our care, we were careful not to get into battles over inessential things. Where lack of control would cause a child anxiety, we often gave way. Lucy, for instance, really didn't like Father Christmas filling her stocking without her knowing what was going in it. So although I thought it spoilt the surprise, I accepted that getting her to help me pack it and put it on her bed made her happy, because there was then no need for her to worry about the contents, or its arrival. On Christmas Day she acts as surprised as the other children, and loves the fact that she is a "little elf" who helps to fill the stockings. Giving Lucy the control she wanted over what to her was a stressful situation has resulted in Christmas Eve being a precious period that we both look forward to, when we spend time together packing her stocking.

What worked?

Sophie – tantrums

Whilst it would be great to say Sophie changed overnight into a happy, loving child, the reality was that she didn't. We would sit with her for hours, often talking gently to soothe her whilst she screamed demands like, 'I want the hat!' hysterically, over and over again. Even when we were happy to give her what she was demanding, it didn't stop the screaming. What were we to do when she had the hat, and was still screaming for it? We gradually accepted that, like her birth parents, she did have learning difficulties, and that these impacted on her understanding and hence her behaviour.

There was also the impact of her dysfunctional early years, and in this respect we had so much to learn. It was like learning a new language: we read books on neglect, Foetal Alcohol Spectrum Disorders, went on courses about attachment, searched the internet for similar stories, and made contact with other adopters going through similar experiences. Gradually, we got there; we treated her at her behavioural age rather than her chronological age, and we learnt to recognise the situations that would be too much for her and would result in a meltdown, and intervened quickly to divert her attention to something she could cope with. More than anything, we accepted Sophie for who she was, realising that with her level of understanding, life was a daily challenge. As soon as we appreciated her difficulties, we were much more able to see and rejoice when we saw progress.

Ben – smashing, stealing and shame

As Ben grew, there were days when open-plan living seemed a real possibility – not through choice, but because he had got angry again and kicked another hole in a wall.

However, we were determined not to give up on Ben.

He had become "our child" because of his horrendous early experiences, and we couldn't reject him because these same early experiences had inevitably affected his behaviour. It wasn't easy though: he stole from family and friends, often taking from those who had, till then, stuck by him – a cousin's MP3 player, his class teacher's phone, a grandparent's money. He then lied ridiculously, even when the items were found in his possession, and destroyed relationships with people who simply did not, or could not, understand his actions.

As time passed, people often told us that his future looked bleak because of his negative behaviours. Our response was that it was all the more important to give him a positive childhood, and counterintuitively we chose to minimise the consequences when he misbehaved. He did know that stealing was wrong and felt ashamed – adding to that shame was not going to stop him. Instead, we did whatever we could to increase his self-esteem and build a healthy relationship with him. We played with him a lot, cuddled him a lot, and since he felt uncomfortable talking about how he felt, we gave him plenty of opportunities to express himself using art.

But we did also talk about feelings by encouraging Ben to describe how he felt when he was, for example, happy, sad or angry, and discussed what he did when he had these feelings and what other actions might have better outcomes. Ben had the capacity to move from calm to rage in milliseconds – teachers were concerned that unlike other children, they did not "see" Ben's anger building: he just erupted. He did not instinctively recognise that he was getting cross, and often seemed as surprised as everyone else with the drama unfolding around him. So we treated him as a much younger child, telling him when he was tired or grumpy, describing to him changes in his behaviour and giving him a choice of activities that would relax and calm him. At home, that meant keeping him close to us and often giving him a simple repetitive task such as sharpening pencils or sorting Lego into boxes. We helped Ben to recognise what happened in his body when he got angry: 'Your breathing usually gets faster and the veins stand out on your neck...', and we encouraged him to take deep breaths when something was worrying him. It helped him, and we would hear him play with Punch and Judy puppets and tell Punch, 'You've got to breathe!' The use of art materials generally was helpful in allowing all the children to work through how they felt – we had many painted volcanoes before we got any rainbows!

We also reduced Ben's opportunities for failing. If we knew it was inevitable that he would find a party or a school trip stressful, he wouldn't go. When outdoors, we kept him under close supervision, and at home we locked away things that he might be tempted to steal. Initially, we feared that he would never develop the ability to self-regulate, but this has not been the case – gradually, he has. In many ways, like his sister, he needed to be treated as a much younger child: kept safe from danger and allowed to learn, and at times inevitably fail, but with our support and encouragement.

What didn't work?

We did feel pressurised, on occasions, by professionals to try common parenting strategies such as star charts to get Ben to behave better, but this was a mistake, for he was not going to be manipulated into doing anything, and it did not build trust between us. He would happily go without a treat rather than feel controlled by someone else. On one occasion, when Ben was being encouraged not to slam a door, we told him that he could have 50p, but every time he slammed the door that day, a penny would be taken off. He proceeded to repeatedly slam the door...50 times; we were not to use that tactic again!

Star charts also particularly stressed him out because of his huge fear of failing and the unbearable shame it brought. It was invariably far better for Ben to destroy the star chart and sabotage the chance of getting a reward, just to get the failure out of the way.

We were keen to work with professionals to obtain help for the children, but were often disillusioned by the assumption that, because the children had problems, we must be having difficulties in parenting. Several times we were surprised to be referred for parenting courses by people who had not even met or discussed the children (or their backgrounds) with us.

Over time, we realised that we were the experts on "our" children, and learnt to trust our instincts about what was best for them. We sat through one session with a professional at which Ben was repeatedly asked if he had nightmares. 'No,' he replied each time. Eventually, the professional asked 'But if you were to have nightmares, what would they be about?' As Ben looked increasingly frustrated, the professional proceeded to ask Ben if he thought he might be taken away from us. Ben looked horrified, and again he answered 'No'. We are confident that the thought had not seriously crossed Ben's mind – at least, until that moment. After all, we had always stressed to the children that we were "together forever". Ben was incredibly unsettled for weeks after this session, scared to let us out of his sight. We have made sure he would never be put through such an ordeal again.

Enjoying the challenge

Like many adopted children, ours have a large birth family, and when two younger siblings also needed a new family, they too became part of ours. Our children had known about them since their births, and were very enthusiastic about living together. Unfortunately, they had to wait until their siblings were of school age before they could join us, and there were to be new challenges ahead.

Harry

Out of all our children, Harry had spent the greatest amount of time in the care of his birth parents, and he sought to re-create that environment in our home. He urinated up walls and seemed to like the smell. His foster carer had warned us that he would manipulate situations to cause an argument, and then sit back and watch. This certainly proved to be the case, and we had to be vigilant that he didn't upset the other children. He also struggled with food – if food was available, then he was going to eat it. He either didn't know or didn't care if he was full; his survival tactics had taught him that when food was there you ate it.

Harry was also extremely destructive. All our children had more than the usual number of accidents with their toys: planes whose wings fell off, dolls whose hair fell out or whose heads just came off. But Harry took things to a new dimension – every soft toy had the stuffing pulled out "by accident"! Every other toy was destined to fall apart or mysteriously malfunction. Naturally, we questioned why

89

he did this. Was it low self-esteem that meant he didn't think himself worthy of nice things? Was he mimicking the behaviour he had witnessed in his birth family? Was he showing his pent-up anger? We repeatedly told him that we thought he was adorable, and emphasised how he could have and enjoy nice things. Gradually, his teddies were subjected to fewer "operations".

Delighted that Harry seemed to have moved on from his early destructive behaviour and that he now wanted nice things for himself, we said he could have the newly decorated bedroom with the soft carpet that all the children secretly coveted. But within days the pristine walls were covered by what looked like slimy snail trails. He had spat on all of the walls, watching the spit run down. The carpet had numerous bare patches where he had used a knitting needle to pull out the threads. Again, we were forced to see that our children's behaviours were very deeply ingrained. Harry had no idea why he had done it. However, time, along with a lot of love and patience, did begin to heal him, and four years later Harry is proud of his new bedroom. He will even sometimes ask me to look after a toy or two so he doesn't scrape the wall with them if he gets cross.

Daniel

Daniel had been attached to his foster carer – it was clear from watching him jump into her arms during introductions. The early days were difficult, as we tried to get to know him and he withdrew from any physical contact and would avoid eye contact at all costs. Gradually though, and on his terms, he came round: one day, as I was sitting down, he came up behind me and threw his arms around my neck, hugging my back. Daniel has gone on to be the most affectionate of children.

His closeness to his foster carer and his caution in responding to us, which I had been so worried about initially, actually demonstrated an ability to form healthy attachments.

Siblings – a good thing

Ensuring that the two younger boys were accepted by their older siblings was never a problem. We had told them about their younger brothers as soon as they were born. But they found it hard that they were no longer babies when they joined us. Nevertheless, they very quickly gelled together.

We soon worked out who wound up whom and which combination of children played nicely together, and incorporated this into our daily lives. So, for example, Ben would sit next to Daniel but not Harry at the meal table, and would sit next to Sophie but not Lucy in the car. This structure was crucial to relieve the children's stress. Knowing who sat next to whom was one less thing for them to worry about.

We made a real effort to give each child quality time with us to talk or just feel special. It wasn't always a big trip out, and could be as simple as Harry walking to the bakery on a Saturday morning with Daddy, or Ben helping me to clean out the rabbits, but it was important that they each had this time regularly without the other children around.

Although the children all had emotional and behavioural difficulties, and people sometimes questioned our sanity when we adopted again, we found that in some ways it made things easier: if one child was being difficult, the fact that other children were progressing motivated

SECTION II

us to keep going; and on days when they all seemed to struggle, the variety of their difficulties meant that we were not all-consumed by one issue and could keep things in perspective.

School

School was a challenge for us all, teachers included. For the children there were so many perceived threats – in the early days they would hide under tables, throw toys, bring things home that weren't theirs, shout, swear and hit other children. As parents we would do the "walk of shame" across the playground as their class teachers came out and made eye contact that invariably said 'Your child has been terrible and I need to talk to you… again!' As the children grew, so did the challenges. The Lego piece brought home in the pocket became a mobile phone squirreled away in a bag; the hiding under a table became running out of class or even out of school.

When Sophie started school she continually took other girls' hair clips. Eventually, the head teacher decided that she would check Sophie's hair and bag at the end of each day to 'help her make sure she didn't have any that weren't hers'. On the first day of this new action plan, the head teacher was delighted that Sophie didn't seem to have any hair clips. I was surprised that the head teacher thought her intervention had been sufficient to stop Sophie stealing, and had to laugh when, helping Sophie to change out of her school uniform, I came across at least a dozen clips attached to the belt of her pinafore under her jumper! Although Sophie did continue to take things and would sometimes come home wearing other children's clothes under her school shirt (often chewing used gum she'd picked up off the pavement!), we realised she wasn't doing something wrong intentionally – we felt it was a natural response to her early neglect, and that she should not have to face the consequences. Instead, we taught her about hygiene and told her endlessly how lovely she was, and how she didn't need to take things because we would look after her and provide for her needs. Gradually, her self-esteem grew.

Unfortunately, Sophie often got far less attention than she needed at school. She reserved her tantrums for us at home. In the classroom she was quiet, seeking to avoid any demands being made on her by fading into the background. Professionals told us that we should take it as a compliment, for it showed that she felt secure enough with us to show us how she felt. (We often wished that she paid us fewer compliments!) But at school the fact that she was not disruptive made it all too easy for teachers just to leave her alone. Meanwhile, in the playground she found peer relationships very difficult to understand, and would spend time in her own little world, or on the fringe of groups of children where she was more tolerated than accepted. What her teachers didn't realise was that her quietness hid an inability to understand much of the teaching, and that her difficulties with social skills left her vulnerable to being bullied. We helped her where we could: paying for extra tuition, encouraging her to attend clubs, inviting children round to play. Some teachers from her school did go on courses at the Post-Adoption Centre in London about meeting the needs of adopted children in school, but perhaps most helpful to her was a charismatic teaching assistant who happened to be an adopted person herself, and who told Sophie how she was special, like her.

Now almost sixteen, Sophie still struggles with learning, but is not only following a normal timetable during the school day but has chosen to do an art GCSE as an extra subject after school. She is also managing to complete her bronze Duke of Edinburgh's Award by working with a group of other children. Meanwhile, her tantrums at home have become a rarity that only serve to remind us of how far she has come.

For Lucy, school has also been difficult. We home-educated her for a term at the end of Year 6 when the pressure of tests and the prospect of going on a residential school trip resulted in daily tears and tantrums. It was clear that with ADHD and resulting difficulties in concentration, combined with severe dyslexia and dyscalculia, tests were sheer torture for her. Furthermore, the last thing she wanted was to give her peers, who often teased her for being bottom of the class, the opportunity to discover that she also sleep-walked and had night terrors.

It was the right decision to teach her at home, and Lucy's behaviour improved immediately when the pressure of school was removed. She spent an enjoyable term learning about how special she was, with days spent in the countryside or at the beach, where she could actively learn about the natural environment without fear of failure.

We did send Lucy to secondary school though, and although it is often fraught, she needs the social interaction with other children. She doesn't have "friends" as such. In fact, as she has grown up, the gap has grown between her and the other teenage girls who happily chat to each other in a way that she cannot comprehend. But she plays football with the boys, and we encourage her love of sport, where she wins approval for her sheer enthusiasm if not her ability, which in turn boosts her self-esteem.

Harry loves school but often finds the social side hard to understand; feeling immense hurt and rejection if a child he likes decides to play with someone else. He is enthusiastic about having friends and often tries to impress his peers by inventing stories about his life. He has, for example, supposedly broken most bones in his body, including his neck! However, in many other ways he acts like any other eleven-year-old boy: we are often amused that he now enjoys the reassurance of a hug and kiss from Mum or Dad as he leaves us at the school gates in the morning, but then quickly scours the area to check that none of his friends have witnessed it!

Daniel, meanwhile, enjoys school, makes friends easily and has been described by his teacher as a joy to teach. He struggles considerably with maths but does not let it bother him and has declared he wants to be a teacher one day. Daniel's school experience has not been without incident – he still remembers his upset feelings at being called a vampire by the other children at four years of age when, as a result of his early neglect, he had to have all his front teeth removed, leaving just his canines. However, he is a happy, resilient child, and simply does not display the emotional and behavioural difficulties of his siblings.

Out of all our children, Ben has definitely had the more obvious difficulties with school. His hyper-vigilance and need to know everything that was going on around him resulted in his schoolwork suffering, as it was not his primary focus. Any unexpected change in routine (often something so small as to be imperceptible to the rest of the class) would increase his stress levels and his behaviour would become ever more challenging: shrieking in class, shouting obscenities and throwing things. His behaviour increasingly alienated him from most of the children, who didn't understand why he was acting as he did. He was drawn into friendships with children who also had behavioural problems, which further exacerbated his own difficulties. He soaked up any deviant behaviour they exhibited like a sponge, repeating new swear words again and again at home, and competing with them for attention in the classroom.

Ben's primary school was actually incredibly important to him, and we worked with the staff to keep him there. His often attention-seeking behaviour could not simply be ignored, because it just increased until he was acknowledged. Rather, it was a case of finding something positive he could get attention for, like his creative artwork or success at a sporting activity. We all had a lot to learn; the school learnt to let him run out of a classroom rather than trying to stop him – making sure he was in sight but not chasing after him, which would only have exacerbated his behaviour. We all learnt that when he was stressed and anxious, there was no point discussing what he had done and what would happen until he was calm, and that was often best left to another day.

Ben not only finished primary school, but finished on a high note with a major part in a school play. In fact, his head teacher, on showing someone round the school, actually said that seeing how far he had come made her job worthwhile, and that Ben's triumph in the play was a visible demonstration of success. Only two years earlier, I had gone to watch his class sing some songs in front of a few parents: at that stage he couldn't cope, and had to be supported by myself and two teaching assistants to prevent him shouting out or running off around the school.

Secondary school was to prove more problematic again for Ben. While at primary school he always had the same class teacher, but at secondary school there was a different teacher for every lesson – 19 in the course of a week – and it was simply too much for him. It seemed that many of the more confident teachers were able to see beyond his apparent cockiness, the loud answering back and disregard for rules, and they won his trust by praising his work. Furthermore, they avoided criticising him, preferring to tell him how well he could do. Less confident teachers, however, appeared to view him as a threat to their control of the class. They shouted at him, argued with him, and invariably eventually excluded him from their lessons. Ben would return home from school stressed and angry. He really could not see where he was at fault. Often he had just asked "another" question loudly, or just been five minutes late for class because he had "needed" to get a drink first, and as far as he was concerned, the teacher was totally wrong and therefore he had every right to tell him so...

Because of the number of staff involved in Ben's care at secondary school, it was impossible to make sure that everyone knew how to handle him. There was one situation when he fled from a lesson because he felt picked on by a teacher, and was chased down a corridor by another teacher who clapped loudly behind his head in a desperate attempt to get his attention. What the teachers did not know was that Ben had probably been hit around the head in the past, so it is perhaps unsurprising that he panicked and proceeded to kick this teacher and to "earn" yet another fixed period exclusion. After several exclusions we took the difficult decision to home-school Ben. Although we thought it had the potential to reduce his stress levels and thereby improve his behaviour, we didn't envisage quite how successful this would be. He is now able to learn because he is in an environment where he feels safe and contained (in a positive way), rather than the huge sensory bombardment of secondary school which left him totally dysregulated. He is spending time at home with well-attuned people and slowly, but successfully, learning to self-regulate. Ben is clearly happier and this has resulted in a much calmer home, which has hugely benefited his siblings.

In the community

We looked forward to the school holidays as a welcome break from the stress that school caused our children and a reduction in difficult behaviour. But there was still the need for structure and the change involved in actually going away from home on a holiday was very unsettling. On arriving at one holiday site, Ben walked around it swearing loudly at everyone. Someone asked us if he had Tourette's Syndrome because of his repetitive shouting out of obscenities. Although it was deeply embarrassing for us at the time, it also showed the level of stress he felt and we are relieved that although he often goes for a long walk if he feels wound up, he now does so quietly.

Part of the problem has always been that all our children look absolutely normal. Their emotional issues related to

SECTION II

their early trauma are not visible. People just see their behaviour, and judge accordingly. As a result, we have sometimes attended meet-ups, and gone on holiday, with other adoptive families from our local authority and further afield, where the children can meet with other adopted children and feel "normal" and where there is a greater understanding of their difficulties and very helpful mutual support.

Contact with the birth family

The children have no direct contact with their birth parents. However, we have a yearly letterbox arrangement with them, which involves social services forwarding a letter to them from us with all the children's news, and us receiving a letter from them updating us on theirs.

We did take the opportunity of meeting the children's birth parents on both occasions that we adopted, and felt that we all benefited from the meetings. For, although the birth parents were not happy with the fact that their children were to be adopted by us, we were able to reassure them that the children would be well cared for. We were also able to find out more information about the children's backgrounds to share with them later.

Has it been worth it?

Recently, I was doing the weekly food shop with Ben, now a fourteen-year-old with fashionably scruffy hair and a charming smile when he chooses to show it. He was carefully packing the shopping into bags, doing well to keep up with the rapid movement of the conveyor belt. He was a joy to be with: sensible, helpful and generally good company, and the shop assistant commented what a great mother I must be to produce a son like this. She gushed forth about the rarity of encountering such a delightful child, and how it had to be a reflection of amazing parenting skills. I caught Ben's eye and we smiled at each other – she had no idea what we had been through together in the previous twelve years and we weren't about to enlighten her. But that evening as I sat watching a film with my husband and Ben, along with four of his siblings, I realised how far we had all come. Looking at each of the children in turn, and knowing how much they had overcome and how many battles they would have ahead of them, I felt proud and protective. Then, looking at my husband and reflecting on the many evenings we had gone to bed exhausted from dealing with the children's behaviours, feeling like we couldn't go on, only to pick up the next day where we had left off, I again felt proud.

You have to have lived through it to understand how difficult life has been, but what had so often seemed impossible had actually happened – we were definitely a happy, if not always a conventional, family.

References

Bomber L (2007) *Inside I'm Hurting*, London: Worth Publishing

Bomber L (2011) *What about me?*, London: Worth Publishing

Cook A, Spinazzola J, Ford J, Lanktree C, Blaustein M, Cloitre M, DeRosa R, Hubbard R, Kagen R, Liautaud J, Mallah K, Olafson E and van der Kolk B (2005) 'Complex trauma in children and adolescents', *Psychiatric Annals*, 35:5, pp 390–398

Golding K and Hughes D (2012) *Creating Loving Attachments*, London: Jessica Kingsley Publishers

Hughes D (2009) *Attachment-Focused Parenting*, New York, NY: WW Norton

Hughes D (2012) *It was that One Moment…*, London: Worth Publishing

Siegel DJ (2011) *The Developing Mind* (2nd ed), New York, NY: Guilford Press

Sroufe LA, Egeland B, Carlson E and Collins WA (2005) *The Development of the Person*, New York, NY: Guilford Press

Useful organisations

Listed below are a short selection of organisations which can provide information and assistance in meeting the needs of children with emotional and behavioural difficulties.

The Anna Freud Centre
Provides services to families and children with emotional, behavioural and developmental difficulties, and also conducts research into the effectiveness of psychotherapy techniques and children's emotional development.
12 Maresfield Gardens
London NW3 5SU
Tel: 020 7794 2313
www.annafreud.org

Association for Child and Adolescent Mental Health
An association for professionals who are involved with children. It

arranges seminars and publishes professional journals, but does not
provide an advice service.
St Saviour's House
39–41 Union Street
London SE1 1SD
Tel: 020 7403 7458
www.acamh.org.uk

British Association for Counselling and Psychotherapy (BACP)

Provides details of local counsellors and psychotherapists.
BACP House, 15 St John's Business Park
Lutterworth
Leicestershire LE17 4HB
Tel: 01455 883300
www.bacp.co.uk

Caspari Foundation (formerly Forum for the Educational Therapy and Therapeutic Teaching, FAETT)

Promotes educational therapy and therapeutic learning to help
children who have emotional barriers that can impair learning.
Provides courses for teachers as well as consultations for children and
parents.
53 Eagle Wharf Road
London N1 7ER
Tel: 020 7704 1977
www.caspari.org.uk

The Centre for Child Mental Health

Aims to increase awareness of emotional well-being and mental health
of children. It conducts research, provides information for parents,
teachers and professionals, and provides seminars on child mental
health topics.
2–18 Britannia Row
London N1 8PA

Tel: 020 7354 2913
www.childmentalhealthcentre.org

Family Futures

An adoption and adoption support agency which specialises in therapeutic work for children who have experienced early trauma and who have attachment difficulties.

3 & 4 Floral Place
7–9 Northampton Grove
London N1 2PL
Tel: 020 7354 4161
www.familyfutures.co.uk